Tell My Story: Germany 1851

Tell My Story Collection, Volume 1

Angeline Gallant

Published by Angeline Gallant, 2021.

While every precaution has been taken in the preparation of this book, the publisher assumes no responsibility for errors or omissions, or for damages resulting from the use of the information contained herein.

TELL MY STORY: GERMANY 1851

First edition. November 9, 2021.

Copyright © 2021 Angeline Gallant.

ISBN: 979-8227523655

Written by Angeline Gallant.

Also by Angeline Gallant

A Dragon's Diary
Dreaming of Dragons

Calling Her Heart
Whisper of the Heart
No Turning Back
Forsake Me Not
Hear My Cry

FORGET ME NOT
Victoria, Ontario's Babies 1894 - 1895

Guardian of the Heart
Fallen Petals

Keeper Of Secrets
A Lady's Secret

Kingston's Love Chronicles
Springtime Promises

Midnight's Awakening
Heart of the Storm
Walking Through The Storm
Walking Through The Storm
Heart of the Storm

Secrets of the Underworld
Deklan's Dragons

Tell My Story Collection
Tell My Story: Germany 1851
Tell My Story: England 1852

The Dervock Legacy
Echoes of Dervock

The Grave Whisperer
Cataraqui United Church Cemetery
Wedding Bells in Kingston, Ontario, Canada 1923
St. Paul's Anglican Churchyard Kingston, Ontario, Canada A-B

St. Paul's Anglican Churchyard, Kingston, Ontario, Canada C - D
St. Paul's Anglican Churchyard, Kingston, Ontario, Canada G - H
St. Paul's Anglican Churchyard, Kingston, Ontario, Canada J - N
St. Paul's Anglican Churchyard, Kingston, Ontario, Canada O - R
St. Paul's Anglican Churchyard, Kingston, Ontario, Canada S - T
St. Paul's Anglican Churchyard, Kingston, Ontario T - Z
Small Graveyards & Burial Grounds: Kingston, Ontario, Canada
Cataraqui United Church Cemetery 1
Cataraqui United Church Cemetery 2
Cataraqui United Church Cemetary 3
Cataraqui United Church Cemetery 4
Cataraqui United Church Cemetery 5
Beth Israel Cemetery
Cataraqui United Church Cemetery 6

The Timeless Veil
Eternal Devotion

The Wolf Whisperer Series
Journey of the Heart
Cry of a Warrior
Wolf Whisperer volumes 1 & 2
Endless White
The Wolf Whisperer volumes 1 & 2

Timeless
The Time Keeper's Sanctuary

Timeless Whispers of Dervock Saga
Secrets of Dervock

Standalone
Winds of Change vol 1-3

Table of Contents

David Hess[1]

Life for David as a Jewish child born in 1790 in Bonn, Germany, would have been shaped by a mix of restrictive social policies, gradual enlightenment, and the strong influence of Jewish community traditions. This period was part of the tail end of the Age of Enlightenment, which brought with it some hope for greater acceptance and equality for Jewish people, but the path was slow and complicated.

Social and Legal Restrictions

Jews in the German states faced significant legal and social restrictions in the late 18th century. They were often excluded from certain trades, unable to own land, and sometimes required to live in designated areas or ghettos. In Bonn, which was part of the Electorate of Cologne (under the Holy Roman Empire until 1801), Jews lived in a very hierarchical and highly restricted society. They faced a "tolerance tax" (similar to other taxes like the Schutzgeld), which allowed them to reside within certain cities or territories but did not offer them the same rights as Christian citizens.

The Influence of the Enlightenment

In the late 1700s, the Enlightenment ideas, with their emphasis on reason, human rights, and individual liberty, began influencing attitudes toward Jews in Germany. Influential thinkers like Moses Mendelssohn, a Jewish philosopher, argued for integration and the intellectual and social participation of Jews in broader society. This period, known as the Haskalah (Jewish Enlightenment), led some German states to consider reforms that could improve Jewish lives, like granting limited civil rights. However, these changes were often more theoretical than practical, and prejudice remained deeply entrenched in German society.

Education and Occupations

Education would have been central to David's upbringing, primarily through religious schooling. Jewish boys like David often received rigorous training in Hebrew, the Torah, and Talmudic study from a young age. Traditional Jewish occupations included roles as merchants, moneylenders, and artisans, especially since many trades and guilds excluded Jews. Given these limitations, Jewish families often maintained a close-knit community life, focusing on faith, family, and community welfare.

Political Shifts and French Influence

In 1794, a few years after David's birth, Bonn and the surrounding regions were occupied by French Revolutionary forces, bringing the ideals of the French Revolution, including the principles of liberté, égalité, fraternité (liberty, equality, fraternity). The French initially emancipated Jews, granting them equal legal rights and allowing them to integrate more fully into society. However, when the French influence waned and the German Confederation took over in 1815, many of these rights were rolled back, returning Jews to a semi-legal status with limited rights.

Religious and Community Life

David's family would have been part of a traditional Jewish community structure, centered around the synagogue and religious practices. Daily life involved adhering to Jewish dietary laws, celebrating festivals like Passover, and observing the Sabbath. Because Jews were often excluded from general society, their cultural and religious institutions became places of support, learning, and identity preservation.

DAVID, AT THREE YEARS old, would have likely been aware of the excitement in his family surrounding the arrival of his younger brother, Salomon, in 1793. In Jewish families of the time, the birth of a child was celebrated with great joy and deep religious significance. For Salomon, this would mean a bris (circumcision ceremony), which took place eight days after birth. This rite of passage would have involved a small celebration attended by family and close members of the Jewish community.

In their early years, David and Salomon would likely grow up in a close-knit environment, where they would rely on family and community for both social and economic support. David, as the older brother, would eventually play a role in helping his younger sibling learn prayers and religious texts, guiding Salomon as he began his own religious studies around age three or four.

AT SEVEN YEARS OLD, David would have likely been thrilled by the arrival of a baby sister, Julie, in 1797. In their traditional Jewish household in Bonn, a daughter's birth was a cherished event, even if not accompanied by the same formal rites as a son's. Family and community members might have visited to offer congratulations and support, celebrating Julie's birth with blessings and shared meals.

As the oldest sibling, David would have begun taking on small responsibilities within the family, including helping his mother care for Julie. He might have helped by watching over her, singing softly to soothe her, or assisting with small household tasks as their parents managed the needs of three young children.

Growing up, David, Salomon, and Julie would likely share a close bond, strengthened by the challenges their family faced due to the restrictions on Jews in Bonn. David's role as the eldest brother may have also included looking out for his younger siblings, especially Julie, as they navigated life in a tightly-knit community with strong family and religious traditions.

AT 19, DAVID MARRIED Jetta Jeannetta on August 23, 1809, in Bonn, marking a significant milestone in his life and symbolizing his transition into adulthood. Marrying relatively young was not uncommon within Jewish communities of the time, where family stability and the continuity of traditions were highly valued. David and Jetta's marriage would have been a carefully considered union, likely arranged or encouraged by their families, who prioritized compatible backgrounds and shared values within the close-knit Jewish community of Bonn.

The wedding itself would have been a deeply meaningful event, filled with religious rituals and symbolic customs. It would have taken place under a chuppah (wedding canopy), symbolizing the new home David and Jetta would build together. Traditional blessings would be recited, and David would break a glass at the end of the ceremony to commemorate the destruction of the Temple in Jerusalem, a reminder of both joy and resilience for the Jewish people.

Starting married life in Bonn in 1809 would have meant adjusting to changing times as well. The influence of Napoleonic reforms had recently shifted local laws, granting more rights and protections to Jews, though these changes were often temporary and inconsistently applied. As David and Jetta began their life together, they would be both hopeful for greater acceptance in society and aware of the social constraints that still surrounded their community.

In their early years of marriage, David and Jetta would work to establish their household, likely in close connection with extended family. For David, marriage meant taking on new responsibilities, not only for his wife but also for the future children they hoped to raise in a challenging but enduring world.

David's wedding attire in 1809 would have likely combined elements of traditional Jewish dress with the fashions of early 19th-century Germany. Given the era's styles, his outfit would have reflected both his community's customs and the evolving trends influenced by Napoleonic Europe. Here's what David may have worn:

Jacket and Waistcoat

David would have worn a dark, fitted frock coat or tailcoat, typical of formal attire for men of the period. This coat would be long, likely reaching mid-thigh, and buttoned in the front, with a high, standing collar. Underneath, he might have worn a waistcoat—likely in a lighter or subtly patterned fabric such as wool or silk—adding both warmth and elegance.

Shirt and Cravat

His shirt would have been a crisp white, with a high collar that framed his face. At his neck, David might have worn a cravat, which was a decorative neck cloth tied in a loose knot or bow, as was popular in Europe at the time. The cravat would add formality to his look and a sense of dignity for the occasion.

Trousers or Breeches

By 1809, trousers were becoming more common than breeches, though breeches (short pants fastened at the knee) were still worn, particularly for formal events. If he wore trousers, they would likely be fitted and dark, made from wool or another durable fabric. If he opted for breeches, he would pair them with knee-high stockings and formal shoes.

Shoes

David's footwear would likely be a pair of black leather shoes with a low heel, possibly fastened with a small buckle or laces. Sturdy yet refined, these shoes would suit the dignity of the wedding ceremony.

Accessories

David might have worn a tallit (prayer shawl) draped over his shoulders during the wedding ceremony. The tallit is typically a rectangular shawl with fringes (tzitzit) at the corners, symbolizing his commitment to Jewish commandments. This traditional garment would add a deeply spiritual touch to his attire, reminding him of his responsibilities within his faith as he took on the role of husband.

Head Covering

It would have been customary for David to wear a kippah (skullcap) or possibly a more formal shtreimel (fur hat), especially if he came from a particularly observant or traditional Jewish family. The head covering served as a sign of respect and humility before God, particularly significant during the sacred wedding rituals.

Ring

In the Jewish wedding tradition, only the groom gives a ring to the bride, symbolizing his commitment. Though David would not wear a wedding ring, the ritual of placing a simple, unadorned gold ring on Jetta's finger would be a focal point of the ceremony.

Outerwear

Given that his wedding took place in August, he would not have required heavy outerwear. However, if the weather was cool, he might have worn a lightweight cloak or shawl to protect against the evening chill, perhaps in dark wool, lending a sense of dignity to his formal attire.

Overall Look

David's appearance would have been a blend of modest elegance, tradition, and respect. His clothing would signal both his social standing and devotion to his heritage, emphasizing formality while embracing meaningful cultural symbols.

AT 22, DAVID BECAME a father with the birth of his son, Moises "Moses" Maurice Hess, on January 21, 1812, in Bonn. This was a significant moment for David and his wife, Jetta, as welcoming a firstborn son marked a major milestone within their family and community. The birth of Moses would bring both joy and a deep sense of responsibility, as David took on the role of nurturing and guiding his child in the traditions and values of their Jewish heritage.

Naming and Bris Ceremony

Following Jewish custom, Moses would have had his bris (circumcision ceremony) on the eighth day after his birth. This ritual is both a religious obligation and a joyous event, drawing family and friends to celebrate the newborn's entry into the covenant of Abraham. At the bris, Moses would be formally given his Hebrew name, symbolizing his spiritual identity within the Jewish community.

Education and Community Life

As Moses grew, David and Jetta would likely prioritize his religious and moral education. David would have introduced him to Hebrew and the basics of Jewish prayer and scripture from a young age, gradually preparing him for further religious study. In a time when Jews were still subject to many restrictions, David's goal would have been to raise Moses with a strong sense of identity and resilience, rooted in their Jewish values and community support.

The Historical Context

Moses's birth came during a period of social and political change. The French had occupied Bonn, bringing reforms that briefly granted equal rights to Jews. By 1812, though, the situation was beginning to shift as German authorities regained control and re-imposed limitations on Jewish rights and freedoms. For David, the uncertainty of these times would have reinforced the importance of family and tradition as a source of stability and identity amidst changing political landscapes.

David's pride in his firstborn would have been matched by his dedication to teaching Moses the skills and values necessary to navigate their complex world. Moses would grow up with a foundation in Jewish teachings, close family bonds, and an awareness of the challenges and responsibilities he would eventually face as part of a minority community in Germany.

———————————

IN 1813, AT 23 YEARS old, David would have experienced a major turning point in European history as German forces, alongside other allies, defeated Napoleon, ending the French occupation. For David and the Jewish community in Bonn, this victory meant the start of significant changes, many of them uncertain. Under French rule, Jews in the Rhineland had enjoyed expanded rights, including the ability to live in cities, own property, and engage in various trades without the harsh restrictions they had previously faced. Napoleon's reforms had offered a glimpse of integration and equality that David's generation might have only dreamed about.

With Napoleon's defeat, however, German states began to reassess these reforms, and a wave of reactionary policies soon spread. The rights that had allowed Jewish families like David's to settle more freely and participate in society were increasingly revoked or limited. The Jewish community would have felt an atmosphere of tension, wondering whether the freedoms gained under French rule would survive or if they would return to the restrictive conditions of the past.

This political shift likely reinforced David's sense of responsibility to his son, Moses, as he contemplated the kind of future he could provide in a society that remained hesitant to fully accept its Jewish citizens. David might have focused on strengthening family bonds and instilling in Moses a strong sense of resilience, foreseeing that his son would grow up in a time when the promise of equality was still fragile.

David's community would likely have been torn between feelings of relief that the Napoleonic Wars were over and anxiety over how German rule would reshape their rights. This time of uncertainty would bring both a reaffirmation of faith and a resolve to persevere as they navigated a society that saw them as outsiders once again.

AT 24, DAVID WELCOMED his second son, Lazarus, born on October 10, 1814. This addition to the family would have brought great joy and, for David, increased his responsibilities as the father of two young sons. The birth of Lazarus not only expanded their family but also reinforced the importance of family unity and resilience amid the shifting social and political landscape following Napoleon's defeat.

As with his first son, David would have introduced Lazarus to Jewish traditions from an early age. A week after his birth, Lazarus would have had his bris, gathering family and community members together to celebrate his entry into the Jewish faith. For David, these moments were likely bittersweet—filled with both pride in raising another son and concern over the challenges his children might face in a society increasingly retracting the rights once granted to Jews under French rule.

By this time, David would have noticed the limitations slowly being imposed again. Social and economic restrictions were once more creeping back into Jewish life in the Rhineland, leaving families like his to adjust their expectations and strengthen their community ties.

David's role as a father, therefore, became one of fostering a sense of identity, unity, and endurance in Moses and Lazarus. He would have placed particular emphasis on their education and religious grounding, hoping to provide them with the knowledge and values they would need to face a future that, while uncertain, would demand both perseverance and pride in their heritage.

WHEN DAVID WAS 27, he and his wife, Jetta, welcomed their third son, Samuel, on May 8, 1817, in Cöln (now Cologne), Germany. By this time, their family had grown significantly, with Samuel joining his older brothers, Moses and Lazarus. The move to Cöln may have offered David better opportunities, as cities like Cologne had relatively vibrant Jewish communities where Jewish merchants, artisans, and tradespeople sought to build lives amidst complex social restrictions.

Samuel's birth would have been celebrated in a traditional bris ceremony, bringing family, friends, and community members together to welcome him into the covenant. The event would also serve as an opportunity to affirm their community bonds, as families gathered to offer blessings, share meals, and strengthen their connections in a time when external pressures made unity essential.

By 1817, post-Napoleonic Germany was well into the Restoration period, when laws were increasingly reverting to restrict Jewish life. The Congress of Vienna in 1815 had already begun curtailing the rights Jews gained under French rule, and restrictions on residence, economic activities, and social status were reintroduced in many German states. David, now raising three sons, would have felt the weight of these societal changes and the impact they could have on his children's futures.

As Samuel grew, David would likely focus even more on preparing his sons for life in a challenging world, emphasizing not only religious education but also practical skills and resilience. With three young boys, David's responsibilities as a father and a provider would have been his foremost priority, guiding them through an uncertain time with pride in their heritage and an awareness of the perseverance their circumstances would require.

WHEN DAVID WAS 35 YEARS old, his brother Bernhard passed away in Düsseldorf, Germany, in 1825. The loss of a sibling would have been a profound event for David, marking a significant moment of grief and reflection within the family. The emotional impact of losing a brother can deeply affect one's sense of identity and family bonds, especially in a close-knit community.

Grief and Mourning

In Jewish tradition, mourning practices, known as shiva, would follow Bernhard's death. The family would observe a week of intense mourning, during which David and other family members would refrain from work and participate in prayer and remembrance. This period allows family and friends to gather, offer condolences, and support one another through shared grief. David would likely have been heavily involved in these rituals, reflecting on the memories of Bernhard and the bond they shared.

Impact on Family Dynamics

David's loss would have ripple effects through his immediate family and his relationship with his children. As a father of three sons—Moses, Lazarus, and Samuel—he may have used this experience to impart lessons about the fragility of life, the importance of family, and the value of honoring loved ones. He would likely emphasize resilience and the necessity of supporting one another during difficult times.

Social Context

In 1825, the broader societal context of David's life would still weigh on his family. The socio-political atmosphere for Jews in Germany remained fraught, with fluctuating levels of acceptance and increasing restrictions. The loss of Bernhard could have also led David to reflect on the importance of their family heritage and identity in facing an uncertain future.

Personal Reflection

At this age, David would be navigating the complexities of his own life while managing the emotional challenges of mourning. This period may have led him to reassess his priorities, focusing on his role as a father and community member. The experience could strengthen his commitment to instilling Jewish values and traditions in his sons while nurturing a sense of unity within the family amidst the backdrop of loss and the challenges of their time.

AT 35 YEARS OLD, DAVID faced another devastating loss when his wife, Jetta, passed away in Köln (Cologne), Germany, on Nov790 in Bonn, Germany, would have been shaped by a mix of restrictive social policies, gradual enlightenment, and the strong influence of Jewish community traditions. This period was part of the tail end of the Age of Enlightenment, which brought with it some hope for greater acceptance and equality for Jewish people, but the path was slow and complicated.

Social and Legal Restrictions

Jews in the German states faced significant legal and social restrictions in the late 18th century. They were often excluded from certain trades, unable to own land, and sometimes required to live in designated areas or ghettos. In Bonn, which was part of the Electorate of Cologne (under the Holy Roman Empire until 1801), Jews lived in a very hierarchical and highly restricted society. They faced a "tolerance tax" (similar to other taxes like the Schutzgeld), which allowed them to reside within certain cities or territories but did not offer them the same rights as Christian citizens.

The Influence of the Enlightenment

In the late 1700s, the Enlightenment ideas, with their emphasis on reason, human rights, and individual liberty, began influencing attitudes toward Jews in Germany. Influential thinkers like Moses Mendelssohn, a Jewish philosopher, argued for integration and the intellectual and social participation of Jews in broader society. This period, known as the Haskalah (Jewish Enlightenment), led some German states to consider reforms that could improve Jewish lives, like granting limited civil rights. However, these changes were often more theoretical than practical, and prejudice remained deeply entrenched in German society.

Education and Occupations

Education would have been central to David's upbringing, primarily through religious schooling. Jewish boys like David often received rigorous training in Hebrew, the Torah, and Talmudic study from a young age. Traditional Jewish occupations included roles as merchants, moneylenders, and artisans, especially since many trades and guilds excluded Jews. Given these limitations, Jewish families often maintained a close-knit community life, focusing on faith, family, and community welfare.

Political Shifts and French Influence

In 1794, a few years after David's birth, Bonn and the surrounding regions were occupied by French Revolutionary forces, bringing the ideals of the French Revolution, including the principles of liberté, égalité, fraternité (liberty, equality, fraternity). The French initially emancipated Jews, granting them equal legal rights and allowing them to integrate more fully into society. However, when the French influence waned and the German Confederation took over in 1815, many of these rights were rolled back, returning Jews to a semi-legal status with limited rights.

Religious and Community Life

David's family would have been part of a traditional Jewish community structure, centered around the synagogue and religious practices. Daily life involved adhering to Jewish dietary laws, celebrating festivals like Passover, and observing the Sabbath. Because Jews were often excluded from general society, their cultural and religious institutions became places of support, learning, and identity preservation.

DAVID, AT THREE YEARS old, would have likely been aware of the excitement in his family surrounding the arrival of his younger brother, Salomon, in 1793. In Jewish families of the time, the birth of a child was celebrated with great joy and deep religious significance. For Salomon, this would mean a bris (circumcision ceremony), which took place eight days after birth. This rite of passage would have involved a small celebration attended by family and close members of the Jewish community.

In their early years, David and Salomon would likely grow up in a close-knit environment, where they would rely on family and community for both social and economic support. David, as the older brother, would eventually play a role in helping his younger sibling learn prayers and religious texts, guiding Salomon as he began his own religious studies around age three or four.

AT SEVEN YEARS OLD, David would have likely been thrilled by the arrival of a baby sister, Julie, in 1797. In their traditional Jewish household in Bonn, a daughter's birth was a cherished event, even if not accompanied by the same formal rites as a son's. Family and community members might have visited to offer congratulations and support, celebrating Julie's birth with blessings and shared meals.

As the oldest sibling, David would have begun taking on small responsibilities within the family, including helping his mother care for Julie. He might have helped by watching over her, singing softly to soothe her, or assisting with small household tasks as their parents managed the needs of three young children.

Growing up, David, Salomon, and Julie would likely share a close bond, strengthened by the challenges their family faced due to the restrictions on Jews in Bonn. David's role as the eldest brother may have also included looking out for his younger siblings, especially Julie, as they navigated life in a tightly-knit community with strong family and religious traditions.

AT 19, DAVID MARRIED Jetta Jeannetta on August 23, 1809, in Bonn, marking a significant milestone in his life and symbolizing his transition into adulthood. Marrying relatively young was not uncommon within Jewish communities of the time, where family stability and the continuity of traditions were highly valued. David and Jetta's marriage would have been a carefully considered union, likely arranged or encouraged by their families, who prioritized compatible backgrounds and shared values within the close-knit Jewish community of Bonn.

The wedding itself would have been a deeply meaningful event, filled with religious rituals and symbolic customs. It would have taken place under a chuppah (wedding canopy), symbolizing the new home David and Jetta would build together. Traditional blessings would be recited, and David would break a glass at the end of the ceremony to commemorate the destruction of the Temple in Jerusalem, a reminder of both joy and resilience for the Jewish people.

Starting married life in Bonn in 1809 would have meant adjusting to changing times as well. The influence of Napoleonic reforms had recently shifted local laws, granting more rights and protections to Jews, though these changes were often temporary and inconsistently applied. As David and Jetta began their life together, they would be both hopeful for greater acceptance in society and aware of the social constraints that still surrounded their community.

In their early years of marriage, David and Jetta would work to establish their household, likely in close connection with extended family. For David, marriage meant taking on new responsibilities, not only for his wife but also for the future children they hoped to raise in a challenging but enduring world.

David's wedding attire in 1809 would have likely combined elements of traditional Jewish dress with the fashions of early 19th-century Germany. Given the era's styles, his outfit would have reflected both his community's customs and the evolving trends influenced by Napoleonic Europe. Here's what David may have worn:

Jacket and Waistcoat

David would have worn a dark, fitted frock coat or tailcoat, typical of formal attire for men of the period. This coat would be long, likely reaching mid-thigh, and buttoned in the front, with a high, standing collar. Underneath, he might have worn a waistcoat—likely in a lighter or subtly patterned fabric such as wool or silk—adding both warmth and elegance.

Shirt and Cravat

His shirt would have been a crisp white, with a high collar that framed his face. At his neck, David might have worn a cravat, which was a decorative neck cloth tied in a loose knot or bow, as was popular in Europe at the time. The cravat would add formality to his look and a sense of dignity for the occasion.

Trousers or Breeches

By 1809, trousers were becoming more common than breeches, though breeches (short pants fastened at the knee) were still worn, particularly for formal events. If he wore trousers, they would likely be fitted and dark, made from wool or another durable fabric. If he opted for breeches, he would pair them with knee-high stockings and formal shoes.

Shoes

David's footwear would likely be a pair of black leather shoes with a low heel, possibly fastened with a small buckle or laces. Sturdy yet refined, these shoes would suit the dignity of the wedding ceremony.

Accessories

David might have worn a tallit (prayer shawl) draped over his shoulders during the wedding ceremony. The tallit is typically a rectangular shawl with fringes (tzitzit) at the corners, symbolizing his commitment to Jewish commandments. This traditional garment would add a deeply spiritual touch to his attire, reminding him of his responsibilities within his faith as he took on the role of husband.

Head Covering

It would have been customary for David to wear a kippah (skullcap) or possibly a more formal shtreimel (fur hat), especially if he came from a particularly observant or traditional Jewish family. The head covering served as a sign of respect and humility before God, particularly significant during the sacred wedding rituals.

Ring

In the Jewish wedding tradition, only the groom gives a ring to the bride, symbolizing his commitment. Though David would not wear a wedding ring, the ritual of placing a simple, unadorned gold ring on Jetta's finger would be a focal point of the ceremony.

Outerwear

Given that his wedding took place in August, he would not have required heavy outerwear. However, if the weather was cool, he might have worn a lightweight cloak or shawl to protect against the evening chill, perhaps in dark wool, lending a sense of dignity to his formal attire.

Overall Look

David's appearance would have been a blend of modest elegance, tradition, and respect. His clothing would signal both his social standing and devotion to his heritage, emphasizing formality while embracing meaningful cultural symbols.

AT 22, DAVID BECAME a father with the birth of his son, Moises "Moses" Maurice Hess, on January 21, 1812, in Bonn. This was a significant moment for David and his wife, Jetta, as welcoming a firstborn son marked a major milestone within their family and community. The birth of Moses would bring both joy and a deep sense of responsibility, as David took on the role of nurturing and guiding his child in the traditions and values of their Jewish heritage.

Naming and Bris Ceremony

Following Jewish custom, Moses would have had his bris (circumcision ceremony) on the eighth day after his birth. This ritual is both a religious obligation and a joyous event, drawing family and friends to celebrate the newborn's entry into the covenant of Abraham. At the bris, Moses would be formally given his Hebrew name, symbolizing his spiritual identity within the Jewish community.

Education and Community Life

As Moses grew, David and Jetta would likely prioritize his religious and moral education. David would have introduced him to Hebrew and the basics of Jewish prayer and scripture from a young age, gradually preparing him for further religious study. In a time when Jews were still subject to many restrictions, David's goal would have been to raise Moses with a strong sense of identity and resilience, rooted in their Jewish values and community support.

The Historical Context

Moses's birth came during a period of social and political change. The French had occupied Bonn, bringing reforms that briefly granted equal rights to Jews. By 1812, though, the situation was beginning to shift as German authorities regained control and re-imposed limitations on Jewish rights and freedoms. For David, the uncertainty of these times would have reinforced the importance of family and tradition as a source of stability and identity amidst changing political landscapes.

David's pride in his firstborn would have been matched by his dedication to teaching Moses the skills and values necessary to navigate their complex world. Moses would grow up with a foundation in Jewish teachings, close family bonds, and an awareness of the challenges and responsibilities he would eventually face as part of a minority community in Germany.

IN 1813, AT 23 YEARS old, David would have experienced a major turning point in European history as German forces, alongside other allies, defeated Napoleon, ending the French occupation. For David and the Jewish community in Bonn, this victory meant the start of significant changes, many of them uncertain. Under French rule, Jews in the Rhineland had enjoyed expanded rights, including the ability to live in cities, own property, and engage in various trades without the harsh restrictions they had previously faced. Napoleon's reforms had offered a glimpse of integration and equality that David's generation might have only dreamed about.

With Napoleon's defeat, however, German states began to reassess these reforms, and a wave of reactionary policies soon spread. The rights that had allowed Jewish families like David's to settle more freely and participate in society were increasingly revoked or limited. The Jewish community would have felt an atmosphere of tension, wondering whether the freedoms gained under French rule would survive or if they would return to the restrictive conditions of the past.

This political shift likely reinforced David's sense of responsibility to his son, Moses, as he contemplated the kind of future he could provide in a society that remained hesitant to fully accept its Jewish citizens. David might have focused on strengthening family bonds and instilling in Moses a strong sense of resilience, foreseeing that his son would grow up in a time when the promise of equality was still fragile.

David's community would likely have been torn between feelings of relief that the Napoleonic Wars were over and anxiety over how German rule would reshape their rights. This time of uncertainty would bring both a reaffirmation of faith and a resolve to persevere as they navigated a society that saw them as outsiders once again.

AT 24, DAVID WELCOMED his second son, Lazarus, born on October 10, 1814. This addition to the family would have brought great joy and, for David, increased his responsibilities as the father of two young sons. The birth of Lazarus not only expanded their family but also reinforced the importance of family unity and resilience amid the shifting social and political landscape following Napoleon's defeat.

As with his first son, David would have introduced Lazarus to Jewish traditions from an early age. A week after his birth, Lazarus would have had his bris, gathering family and community members together to celebrate his entry into the Jewish faith. For David, these moments were likely bittersweet—filled with both pride in raising another son and concern over the challenges his children might face in a society increasingly retracting the rights once granted to Jews under French rule.

By this time, David would have noticed the limitations slowly being imposed again. Social and economic restrictions were once more creeping back into Jewish life in the Rhineland, leaving families like his to adjust their expectations and strengthen their community ties.

David's role as a father, therefore, became one of fostering a sense of identity, unity, and endurance in Moses and Lazarus. He would have placed particular emphasis on their education and religious grounding, hoping to provide them with the knowledge and values they would need to face a future that, while uncertain, would demand both perseverance and pride in their heritage.

WHEN DAVID WAS 27, he and his wife, Jetta, welcomed their third son, Samuel, on May 8, 1817, in Cöln (now Cologne), Germany. By this time, their family had grown significantly, with Samuel joining his older brothers, Moses and Lazarus. The move to Cöln may have offered David better opportunities, as cities like Cologne had relatively vibrant Jewish communities where Jewish merchants, artisans, and tradespeople sought to build lives amidst complex social restrictions.

Samuel's birth would have been celebrated in a traditional bris ceremony, bringing family, friends, and community members together to welcome him into the covenant. The event would also serve as an opportunity to affirm their community bonds, as families gathered to offer blessings, share meals, and strengthen their connections in a time when external pressures made unity essential.

By 1817, post-Napoleonic Germany was well into the Restoration period, when laws were increasingly reverting to restrict Jewish life. The Congress of Vienna in 1815 had already begun curtailing the rights Jews gained under French rule, and restrictions on residence, economic activities, and social status were reintroduced in many German states. David, now raising three sons, would have felt the weight of these societal changes and the impact they could have on his children's futures.

As Samuel grew, David would likely focus even more on preparing his sons for life in a challenging world, emphasizing not only religious education but also practical skills and resilience. With three young boys, David's responsibilities as a father and a provider would have been his foremost priority, guiding them through an uncertain time with pride in their heritage and an awareness of the perseverance their circumstances would require.

WHEN DAVID WAS 35 YEARS old, his brother Bernhard passed away in Düsseldorf, Germany, in 1825. The loss of a sibling would have been a profound event for David, marking a significant moment of grief and reflection within the family. The emotional impact of losing a brother can deeply affect one's sense of identity and family bonds, especially in a close-knit community.

Grief and Mourning

In Jewish tradition, mourning practices, known as shiva, would follow Bernhard's death. The family would observe a week of intense mourning, during which David and other family members would refrain from work and participate in prayer and remembrance. This period allows family and friends to gather, offer condolences, and support one another through shared grief. David would likely have been heavily involved in these rituals, reflecting on the memories of Bernhard and the bond they shared.

Impact on Family Dynamics

David's loss would have ripple effects through his immediate family and his relationship with his children. As a father of three sons—Moses, Lazarus, and Samuel—he may have used this experience to impart lessons about the fragility of life, the importance of family, and the value of honoring loved ones. He would likely emphasize resilience and the necessity of supporting one another during difficult times.

Social Context

In 1825, the broader societal context of David's life would still weigh on his family. The socio-political atmosphere for Jews in Germany remained fraught, with fluctuating levels of acceptance and increasing restrictions. The loss of Bernhard could have also led David to reflect on the importance of their family heritage and identity in facing an uncertain future.

Personal Reflection

At this age, David would be navigating the complexities of his own life while managing the emotional challenges of mourning. This period may have led him to reassess his priorities, focusing on his role as a father and community member. The experience could strengthen his commitment to instilling Jewish values and traditions in his sons while nurturing a sense of unity within the family amidst the backdrop of loss and the challenges of their time.

AT 35 YEARS OLD, DAVID faced another devastating loss when his wife, Jetta, passed away in Köln (Cologne), Germany, on November 28, 1825. The death of a spouse is one of life's most profound tragedies, and this event would have had a profound impact on David and their three sons: Moses, Lazarus, and Samuel.

Grief and Mourning

Following Jetta's death, David would have entered a period of mourning according to Jewish customs. This process, particularly after losing a spouse, is marked by intense sorrow and rituals such as shiva, which lasts for seven days. During this time, David and his children would have refrained from normal daily activities, focusing on remembering Jetta's life, praying, and receiving visitors who came to offer condolences and support.

David's grief would have been compounded by the necessity of taking care of his children, who were still quite young. At this point, Moses would have been 13, Lazarus 11, and Samuel just 8. David would need to find a balance between processing his own profound loss and ensuring that his sons felt supported during this difficult time.

Impact on Family Dynamics

The absence of Jetta would create a void in the family structure. David would now have to take on the dual role of both father and mother, which would likely change the dynamics of their household significantly. He might have leaned more on family and community for support, looking to relatives and friends to help care for his sons and provide guidance.

This loss could also deepen the bond between David and his sons as they navigated their grief together. David would likely emphasize the importance of family unity, teaching his children to lean on one another and support each other through their shared sorrow.

Social Context

In the broader societal context, the years leading up to and following Jetta's death were marked by ongoing challenges for the Jewish community in Germany. After the brief period of emancipation during the Napoleonic Wars, the rights of Jews were increasingly restricted again. This would place additional stress on David as he grappled with his family's grief while navigating a society that remained precarious for Jewish citizens.

Personal Reflection

David's experiences of loss would lead to profound personal reflection. He might have found himself questioning the fragility of life and the importance of leaving a legacy for his children. This period would prompt him to instill in them the values of resilience, faith, and community, ensuring that they carried forward the teachings and traditions of their heritage even in the face of such adversity.

In summary, the loss of Jetta would not only alter the fabric of David's family but would also shape his outlook on life, prompting him to seek strength in his role as a father and as a member of the Jewish community in Köln.

AT 36 YEARS OLD, IN 1826, David would have experienced the advent of safety matches, a significant invention that changed everyday life and household safety. While it's unlikely that the matches available at that time were the modern safety matches we know today, their development marked a pivotal shift in how people ignited fire.

Impact of Matches on Daily Life

1. Convenience and Safety: Prior to the invention of matches, lighting fires was a labor-intensive process that often required flint and steel or a burning brand. The introduction of matches made starting a fire much more convenient, allowing families like David's to light candles, cook food, and heat their homes more easily.

———————

2. DOMESTIC LIFE: FOR a widowed father of three young boys, the availability of matches would have simplified many daily tasks. Lighting the stove for cooking, candles for evening illumination, or fires for warmth would have become quicker and safer, allowing David to focus more on his children and their needs.

———————

3. SOCIAL CHANGES: As matches became more commonplace, social practices and gatherings could have been affected. Lighting candles for Shabbat or other family gatherings would have been less of a chore, allowing David to create a more inviting atmosphere for family and friends.

———————

4. CULTURAL SIGNIFICANCE: Matches would have also played a role in rituals and traditions. For instance, lighting the Shabbat candles or the menorah during Hanukkah would be done more easily, allowing for more focus on the spiritual aspects of these traditions rather than the logistical challenges of lighting them.

———————

REFLECTIONS ON INVENTION and Change

The invention of matches in 1826 occurred in a time of great change and innovation. For David, who was grappling with the loss of his wife and raising three sons in an uncertain social environment, this technological advancement might have offered a sense of progress and hope.

The ease that came with using matches could also have allowed David to reflect on the evolution of household tools and how they impacted the daily lives of families like his own. As he adapted to these changes, David might have viewed the invention of matches as a small but meaningful enhancement to his family's quality of life, offering him the opportunity to create a warm and nurturing home for his children during a challenging period.

In conclusion, the invention of matches would not only have practical implications for David's daily life but could also symbolize a broader trend of innovation and change that he and his sons would navigate together as they moved forward from their recent losses.

WHEN DAVID TURNED 39 in 1829, he faced the significant loss of his father, Nathan David Hess, who passed away in Bonn, Germany. The death of a parent is a deeply impactful event, and for David, this loss would bring a mix of grief, reflection, and responsibility.

Grief and Mourning

1. Mourning Practices: Following Nathan's death, David would observe traditional Jewish mourning practices. The family would likely engage in shiva, a week-long mourning period, where they would gather to remember Nathan and receive visitors who came to offer their condolences. This time would be important not only for honoring his father's memory but also for allowing the family to come together in support of one another during a time of sorrow.

2. REFLECTING ON LEGACY: The loss of his father would lead David to reflect on Nathan's life and teachings. He would consider the values and traditions his father had imparted to him, shaping David's own role as a father to Moses, Lazarus, and Samuel. This period might inspire him to be more intentional in teaching his sons about their heritage and the importance of family, continuity, and Jewish traditions.

IMPACT ON FAMILY DYNAMICS

1. Role of Family: With the passing of Nathan, David would likely feel the weight of being the elder statesman of his family, especially as a widower with three sons. He may have looked to Nathan's example for guidance on how to lead his own family through difficult times, emphasizing the importance of resilience, unity, and support among family members.

2. FATHERLY RESPONSIBILITIES: The loss of Nathan could have heightened David's awareness of the transient nature of life, prompting him to invest even more time and energy into his relationship with his sons. He would strive to create a supportive environment for them, ensuring they felt secure and cared for in light of their collective losses.

SOCIAL CONTEXT

1. Jewish Community: In 1829, the Jewish community in Germany was navigating a complex landscape of rights and restrictions. David would likely engage with the community more actively, seeking

support from fellow Jews who could understand the challenges they faced. The shared experience of mourning could strengthen community ties and provide David and his sons with a sense of belonging.

---

2. POLITICAL LANDSCAPE: The socio-political context during this time continued to pose challenges for Jewish families. As David dealt with his father's death, he would also be aware of the broader implications of their Jewish identity in a society that often treated them as outsiders. This awareness might shape his discussions with his sons about their place in the world and the importance of standing together as a family.

PERSONAL REFLECTION

David's grief over his father's passing would likely lead to profound introspection. He might find himself contemplating his own legacy and what he wanted to pass on to Moses, Lazarus, and Samuel. This reflection could prompt him to prioritize the values of faith, perseverance, and community support, which had been central to his father's life and teachings.

In summary, at 39 years old, David faced the dual challenge of mourning his father while ensuring that his sons felt secure and supported. Nathan's death would serve as a catalyst for David to reaffirm the importance of family bonds, heritage, and resilience in the face of loss, guiding his children through their grief while fostering a strong sense of identity and community.

AT 39 YEARS OLD, DAVID would have witnessed the significant cultural shift that came with the public availability of photography in 1839. This invention marked a new era in visual representation and communication, bringing profound changes to personal, social, and artistic expression.

Impact of Photography on Daily Life

1. Preservation of Memories: The advent of photography offered David and his family a new way to capture and preserve memories. For a man who had experienced considerable loss, including the deaths of his wife and father, having photographs of his children—Moses, Lazarus, and Samuel—would allow him to create lasting memories. Portraits could capture moments of family togetherness, serving as tangible reminders of their life together.

2. RECORD KEEPING: Photography also held practical applications for families, allowing them to document significant events such as birthdays, weddings, and community celebrations. David might have found it valuable to capture milestones in his sons' lives, helping to maintain a sense of continuity in a time when they faced challenges.

3. CONNECTION TO THE Community: As photography became more widely available, it likely facilitated connections within the Jewish community and beyond. David could have commissioned portraits of himself and his sons or participated in community events that involved photography, helping to strengthen social bonds and create shared histories.

SOCIAL AND CULTURAL Context

1. Art and Identity: The rise of photography coincided with a period of artistic experimentation and change. David might have engaged with this new medium as a way to express his identity and that of his family. As a Jewish man in early 19th-century Germany, David could have used photography to assert his family's presence and heritage in a society that often marginalized Jewish identities.

———

2. PUBLIC AND PRIVATE Spheres: Photography blurred the lines between public and private life. David may have embraced the opportunity to showcase his family in a more public setting, which could be empowering, especially as a widower trying to rebuild his family life.

———

3. CULTURAL COMMENTARY: As a member of the Jewish community, David may have recognized the potential for photography to document and comment on social issues. This new medium could be employed to raise awareness of the challenges facing Jewish families, reflecting both the struggles and triumphs of their experiences.

———

PERSONAL REFLECTION

David's exposure to photography might have prompted him to consider how he wanted to be remembered, both by his sons and by the community. With the losses he had endured, he may have felt a desire to capture his family's story visually, using portraits to convey the love and resilience that characterized their lives.

This could have led him to take an active role in ensuring that his sons not only understood their heritage but also had a physical representation of their family history that they could pass on to future generations.

Conclusion

In summary, at 39 years old, David found himself at the intersection of personal loss and societal change. The public availability of photography in 1839 presented an opportunity for him to document his family life, create lasting memories, and assert his identity within the broader cultural context. As he navigated the challenges of fatherhood in a changing world, photography could serve as both a tool for connection and a means of preserving the legacy of his loved ones.

WHEN DAVID TURNED 50 in 1840, he faced the profound loss of his mother, Eva Scheva Susmann Seltzer, in Bonn. This significant event would have brought both emotional weight and reflection as he navigated his life in the context of family, heritage, and the changes occurring in society.

Grief and Mourning

1. Loss of a Matriarch: The passing of Eva would have been particularly impactful for David, as mothers often hold a central role in family dynamics. David may have felt a deep sense of grief and responsibility, reflecting on the teachings, traditions, and values that his mother had imparted to him throughout his life.

2. MOURNING CUSTOMS: Following Eva's death, David would likely have engaged in Jewish mourning rituals, including shiva. This

period of mourning would involve gathering family and friends to honor Eva's memory, share stories, and offer support. David's sons—Moses, Lazarus, and Samuel—would witness this communal support, reinforcing the importance of family and tradition.

REFLECTION ON FAMILY Legacy

1. Passing Down Traditions: With the loss of his mother, David might have felt a renewed urgency to pass on Jewish traditions and values to his sons. He could have used this time to share stories about his mother's life and her influence on their family, ensuring that her memory lived on through the next generation.

---

2. PARENTAL GUIDANCE: At this stage in life, David would be well aware of the challenges of raising his sons without the support of their grandmother. He may have taken a more active role in their upbringing, drawing on the lessons he learned from Eva to instill values such as compassion, resilience, and the importance of community.

SOCIAL AND CULTURAL Context

1. Jewish Community in Transition: The 1840s were a time of both change and challenge for Jewish communities in Europe. David would have been acutely aware of the social dynamics affecting Jews in Germany, including the struggle for rights and acceptance. This awareness could have influenced how he communicated with his sons about their identity, encouraging them to embrace their heritage while navigating a complex social landscape.

---

2. CULTURAL SIGNIFICANCE of Mourning: The death of a prominent community member, like Eva, might have been significant not only for the family but also for the wider Jewish community. David's family could have received support and condolences from their neighbors, reflecting the interconnectedness of the Jewish community in Bonn.

PERSONAL REFLECTION

As David grieved his mother's death, he may have found himself contemplating the passage of time and his own mortality. At 50, he was at a point in life where he could reflect on the legacies he wished to leave for his sons. This contemplation might have prompted him to consider how he could best honor his mother's memory, whether through storytelling, traditions, or ensuring his children remained connected to their Jewish roots.

David could have also felt a sense of duty to maintain familial connections, perhaps reaching out to relatives or community members to reinforce the bonds that had been central to his upbringing. In this way, he could create a living tribute to Eva by ensuring that her values and lessons continued to resonate within the family.

Conclusion

In summary, at the age of 50, David faced the significant loss of his mother, which would have led to deep personal reflection and a renewed commitment to his family and heritage. The mourning process would have offered an opportunity for communal support and connection, allowing David to honor Eva's memory while navigating the challenges of parenting and cultural identity in a rapidly changing society. Through this journey, David would aim to ensure that the legacy of his mother, and the values she embodied, continued to influence the lives of his sons.

AT 55 YEARS OLD, DAVID experienced the sorrowful loss of his brother, Salomon, in 1845 in Bonn. This event would have had profound emotional, familial, and cultural implications for David as he continued to navigate his life in a changing society.

Grief and Mourning

1. Sibling Bond: The death of Salomon would have been particularly impactful for David, as siblings often share a unique bond forged through shared childhood experiences and family dynamics. David likely experienced a deep sense of grief, reflecting on their shared past and the memories they created together. This loss might have been a stark reminder of the fragility of life and the importance of familial connections.

---

2. JEWISH MOURNING Rituals: Following Salomon's passing, David would likely observe traditional Jewish mourning customs, including shiva, during which family and friends gather to offer support and remember the deceased. This period would provide David an opportunity to connect with his extended family and community, reinforcing the importance of shared grief and mutual support.

FAMILY DYNAMICS

1. Strengthening Family Ties: David might have felt a renewed sense of responsibility to support the remaining members of his family, particularly in the wake of losing another close relative. He may have

sought to bring his remaining siblings, children, and any extended family members together to honor Salomon's memory and provide comfort in their shared loss.

———

2. IMPACT ON HIS SONS: David's grief would have been visible to his sons—Moses, Lazarus, and Samuel—offering them a lesson in the realities of life, love, and loss. David might have used this opportunity to impart values of empathy, resilience, and the importance of family, encouraging his sons to support one another in times of hardship.

———

SOCIAL AND CULTURAL Context

1. Jewish Community Support: Salomon's death would likely have resonated beyond David's immediate family, affecting their local Jewish community. David may have received condolences and support from neighbors, friends, and community members, reinforcing the collective nature of grief within their cultural context.

———

2. CHANGING LANDSCAPE: The mid-19th century was a time of social change for Jewish communities in Europe, marked by struggles for rights and integration into broader society. David, as he dealt with the loss of his brother, would be aware of these challenges, perhaps feeling a sense of solidarity with other families who were navigating similar experiences of loss and adaptation.

———

PERSONAL REFLECTION

At 55, David may have been reflecting on his own life and the legacy he wished to leave behind as he faced yet another loss. The passing of Salomon could have prompted him to consider the impact of his own mortality on his family. He might have thought about how he could preserve the memory of his brother and ensure that Salomon's values and stories were shared with his children.

David may have felt a growing sense of urgency to document their family history and experiences, ensuring that the stories of his brothers, their childhood, and their shared family traditions would continue to resonate with future generations. This could lead him to gather family stories and perhaps even consider how he might commemorate Salomon's life in a way that honored their bond.

Conclusion

In summary, at the age of 55, David faced the significant loss of his brother Salomon, prompting a deep reflection on family, grief, and the bonds that hold them together. Through the mourning process and the support of the community, David would navigate this sorrowful chapter of his life, drawing strength from his remaining family and reinforcing the importance of connection, memory, and shared heritage amidst the challenges of an evolving society.

WHEN DAVID TURNED 56 in 1846, the world was undergoing significant technological advancements, one of which was the invention of the sewing machine, patented by Elias Howe. This invention not only revolutionized the garment industry but also had broader implications for society, particularly for families and communities like David's.

Technological Advancement: The Sewing Machine

1. Impact on Clothing Production: The sewing machine drastically changed how clothing was made, allowing for faster and more efficient production. This innovation meant that clothing could be produced in greater quantities and with improved precision. For David's family, this might have meant access to more affordable and varied clothing options, contributing to their comfort and social status.

---

2. ECONOMIC OPPORTUNITIES: The sewing machine also opened up new economic avenues for individuals, especially women. As more households could now produce garments, it might have led to increased opportunities for women to work from home, either sewing for their families or engaging in small-scale garment production for sale. This could have influenced how David viewed the roles of women in society and the economy.

SOCIETAL CHANGES AND Gender Roles

1. Changing Roles of Women: As sewing became easier and quicker, it may have contributed to a shift in societal expectations around women's labor. With the ability to produce garments more efficiently, women might have had more time to engage in other activities, including education and community involvement. David may have observed these shifts in his own household or community, particularly as he raised his sons.

---

2. DAVID'S FAMILY DYNAMICS: As a father of three sons, David may have had to navigate the changing perceptions of women's roles within his family. While he likely held traditional views shaped by his upbringing, the technological advancements could have prompted him

to consider the broader implications of these changes for his children's futures.

REFLECTION ON PERSONAL Circumstances

1. Adapting to Change: At 56, David may have found himself in a period of reflection about his own life, family, and the changing world around him. The sewing machine could symbolize a broader trend of industrialization and modernization that was sweeping across Europe. He may have wondered how these changes would affect his family's future and their ability to adapt to new societal norms.

---

2. LEGACY AND MEMORY: With the loss of several close family members in recent years, including his brother Salomon and his mother Eva, David may have felt a strong desire to preserve family traditions while also embracing new innovations. He might have thought about how to blend the old ways with the new, ensuring that his children understood their heritage while also preparing them for a modernizing world.

COMMUNITY AND CULTURAL Context

1. Jewish Community Adaptation: As a member of the Jewish community, David would have seen how technological advancements like the sewing machine impacted not only his family but also the broader Jewish community in Bonn. This change could have led to new forms of community engagement, including collaborations in garment production or trade.

---

2. CULTURAL EXCHANGE: The increased production capabilities afforded by the sewing machine might have facilitated cultural exchanges as clothing styles became more accessible. David's family may have begun to wear garments that reflected broader European trends, influencing their cultural identity while maintaining Jewish traditions.

CONCLUSION

In summary, turning 56 in 1846 placed David at the intersection of personal reflection and societal change, marked by the invention of the sewing machine. As he navigated the implications of this technological advancement, he would have had to consider its impact on his family dynamics, the roles of women, and the evolving landscape of his Jewish community. This period in David's life would be characterized by a blend of honoring the past while embracing the possibilities that lay ahead in an ever-changing world.

DAVID'S PASSING AT the age of 62 on December 19, 1851, in Köln (Cologne), Germany, marked the end of a life deeply intertwined with the significant historical, cultural, and social changes of the early 19th century. Reflecting on his life and its context can provide insights into the experiences and challenges he faced, as well as how his death may have impacted his family and community.

Life Overview

1. A Life of Change: Born in 1790, David lived through a transformative period in Europe characterized by the aftermath of the French Revolution, the rise and fall of Napoleon, and the beginnings of industrialization. As a Jewish man in Germany, he experienced both

the challenges and opportunities presented by these changes, navigating societal expectations and cultural shifts.

---

2. FAMILY MAN: THROUGHOUT his life, David married Jetta Jeannetta and raised several children, including Moses, Lazarus, and Samuel. His family was central to his identity, and the losses he experienced—including the deaths of his wife and brother—would have shaped his later years, leading him to reflect on legacy and familial bonds.

DEATH AND MOURNING

1. Cultural Context of Mourning: David's passing would have prompted traditional Jewish mourning practices within his family and community. His children, especially Moses, Lazarus, and Samuel, would likely observe shiva, a seven-day mourning period, where family and friends would gather to share memories and offer support.

---

2. IMPACT ON HIS SONS: David's death would have been a significant loss for his sons, marking a pivotal moment in their lives. They would have to navigate the grief while also considering their roles within the family and the Jewish community. David's teachings, values, and memories would have shaped their paths moving forward.

COMMUNITY RESPONSE

1. Support from the Jewish Community: As a respected member of the Jewish community in Köln, David's passing would likely be felt deeply.

Community members would come together to support his family, reflecting the communal bonds that characterize Jewish life. This support would be crucial in helping his family cope with their loss.

---

2. COMMEMORATION OF David's Life: In the wake of his death, it is possible that David's contributions to his family and community would be recognized through memorial gatherings, where stories of his life and legacy would be shared. His experiences, values, and the lessons he imparted would likely be passed down to his descendants, reinforcing the importance of familial and cultural heritage.

LEGACY

1. Family Legacy: David's life story would be woven into the fabric of his family's history. His children and grandchildren would carry on the traditions, stories, and values he instilled in them. The challenges and triumphs he faced would serve as a source of inspiration and guidance for future generations.

---

2. CULTURAL IMPACT: As society continued to evolve, the values and teachings of figures like David would play a role in shaping the cultural identity of Jewish families in Germany. His experiences navigating the complexities of life in a changing world would resonate with others facing similar challenges.

CONCLUSION

David's death in 1851 at the age of 62 symbolizes the end of a life rich in experiences, marked by personal and communal transformations. As his family and community mourned his passing, they would reflect on the impact he had on their lives and the legacy he left behind. His story serves as a testament to the resilience of individuals and families navigating the ever-changing landscapes of their time, highlighting the importance of memory, community, and continuity in the face of loss.

Moises "Moses" Hess[2]

When Moses "Maurice" Hess was born in Bonn, Germany, on January 21, 1812, the city and the surrounding region were experiencing significant social, political, and cultural changes. Here's an overview of what life was like in Bonn during that period:

Historical Context

1. Post-Napoleonic Era: Bonn was emerging from the upheaval of the Napoleonic Wars (1803–1815). The area had been part of the French Empire under Napoleon, which altered local governance and laws. After Napoleon's defeat, the Congress of Vienna in 1815 redefined European borders and political structures, impacting Bonn's status and its governance as part of the Kingdom of Prussia.

2. POLITICAL LANDSCAPE: The early 19th century was marked by rising nationalism and liberal movements across Europe. In Bonn, as in other German cities, there was a growing sentiment for German unification and democratic reforms, alongside ongoing tensions with the conservative powers that emerged from the Congress of Vienna.

DAILY LIFE

1. Urban Environment: Bonn, the former capital of the Electorate of Cologne, was a vibrant urban center with a rich cultural heritage. The city had a mix of medieval and modern influences, with notable architecture such as the Bonn Minster and the Electoral Palace. Daily life would have included bustling markets, shops, and community gatherings.

2. JEWISH COMMUNITY: Moses was born into a Jewish family in a time when Jews faced various legal restrictions and social discrimination. While some rights had been gained during the Napoleonic era, Jews in Bonn still faced challenges,

including limitations on certain professions and participation in public life. However, the Jewish community remained active in trade, commerce, and cultural life, often maintaining a close-knit community.

---

3. EDUCATION AND RELIGION: Religious education was significant in Jewish families, and children like Moses would likely have been taught Hebrew and Jewish texts, alongside secular subjects if permitted. The community held traditional religious practices and celebrated Jewish festivals, which fostered a strong sense of identity.

ECONOMIC CONDITIONS

1. Trade and Commerce: Bonn was strategically located along the Rhine River, which facilitated trade and commerce. Local businesses included textiles, crafts, and food markets, providing opportunities for families like the Hess family to engage in various trades.

---

2. AGRICULTURAL INFLUENCES: The surrounding areas of Bonn were largely agricultural, with many residents involved in farming and related activities. This agricultural backdrop influenced the local economy and lifestyle, contributing to the community's food supply and trade.

CULTURAL LIFE

1. Cultural and Intellectual Movements: The early 19th century was a period of Romanticism in Germany, emphasizing emotion, nature, and individualism. Bonn was home to several prominent figures in literature and philosophy, including the composer Ludwig van Beethoven, who was born there. This cultural atmosphere would have influenced local society, fostering a vibrant intellectual environment.

---

2. COMMUNITY EVENTS: Festivals, fairs, and public celebrations were common, allowing residents to engage socially and culturally. Music, art, and literature played

significant roles in community life, with opportunities for public performances and gatherings.

CONCLUSION

In summary, when Moses "Maurice" Hess was born in Bonn in 1812, he entered a world marked by the remnants of the Napoleonic Wars, a burgeoning sense of nationalism, and a dynamic cultural landscape. Growing up in a Jewish family in this context, he would have navigated the complexities of identity, community, and the socio-political challenges of his time, all while being influenced by the rich cultural heritage of Bonn.

MOSES "MAURICE" HESS was two years old when his brother Lazarus was born on October 10, 1814, in Bonn. Here's a brief overview of the family dynamics and the broader context during that time:

Family Dynamics

1. Growing Family: With the birth of Lazarus, the Hess family grew larger. Moses, being the older brother, would have begun to take on a role in helping care for his younger sibling. This dynamic often fosters a sense of responsibility and bonding between siblings.

---

2. PARENTAL INFLUENCE: David and Jetta Jeannetta Hess would likely be focused on raising their children in a nurturing environment, instilling cultural and religious values that were important within the Jewish community. The family structure would emphasize education, religious practices, and support for one another.

---

3. SIBLINGS' BONDING: As Moses grew, his relationship with Lazarus would evolve, and their interactions would contribute to their identities. The presence of another brother may have fostered camaraderie, playfulness, and possibly rivalry, common among siblings.

BROADER CONTEXT IN Bonn (1814)

1. Post-Napoleonic Changes: The year 1814 marked the end of the Napoleonic Wars, with the defeat of Napoleon and the reshaping of Europe at the Congress of Vienna. Bonn, like other cities in Germany, was experiencing significant political and social changes, transitioning from French rule back to Prussian control.

---

2. ECONOMIC CONDITIONS: The economy in Bonn would be in a state of recovery following the war. There would have been a mix of opportunities in trade and agriculture, contributing to the livelihood of families in the area, including the Hess family.

---

3. JEWISH COMMUNITY: The Jewish community in Bonn was navigating the aftermath of the wars. The community would still face challenges, such as discrimination and restrictions, but there were also emerging opportunities for greater integration into broader society.

---

4. CULTURAL VIBRANCY: Bonn remained a culturally vibrant city, home to intellectual movements and artistic endeavors. This environment would likely influence the upbringing of Moses and Lazarus, exposing them to music, literature, and ideas that shaped the early 19th century.

CONCLUSION

In summary, the early years of Moses and the arrival of his brother Lazarus in 1814 were shaped by family dynamics and the socio-political context of post-Napoleonic Bonn. The environment would foster a sense of community and cultural richness, even as challenges persisted for the Jewish population. Their childhood experiences would play a significant role in shaping their identities and future paths.

MOSES "MAURICE" HESS was five years old when his brother Samuel was born in Cöln (Cologne), Germany, on May 8, 1817. Here's an overview of family dynamics and the broader context during that time:

Family Dynamics

1. Family Expansion: With Samuel's birth, the Hess family continued to grow. At five years old, Moses would likely have been aware of the changes a new sibling brought to the household, including the additional responsibilities and dynamics that come with having another brother.

2. ROLE AS AN OLDER Brother: As the eldest child, Moses might have felt a sense of pride and responsibility for his younger siblings. He would have had the opportunity to bond with Samuel, likely engaging in play and helping care for him as he grew.

3. SUPPORTIVE ENVIRONMENT: David and Jetta Jeannetta Hess would have focused on creating a nurturing environment for their children. They would be passing down Jewish traditions and cultural values, instilling a sense of community and identity in their growing family.

BROADER CONTEXT IN Cöln (Cologne) (1817)

1. Political Climate: By 1817, the Congress of Vienna had established a new order in Europe following the Napoleonic Wars, including the restoration of Prussian control over the region. This period was characterized by efforts to stabilize Europe politically and socially, but it also saw rising nationalist sentiments and demands for liberal reforms.

2. JEWISH COMMUNITY: The Jewish community in Cöln, like in Bonn, faced ongoing challenges, including restrictions on professions and social discrimination. However, there were also movements towards emancipation, with increased advocacy for Jewish rights beginning to emerge in the 1820s and 1830s.

3. ECONOMIC CONDITIONS: The economy in Cöln was recovering from the impact of war. Trade and commerce were important for the city, benefiting from its strategic location on the Rhine River. The Hess family would have engaged in economic activities reflective of the local context, potentially in trade or crafts.

4. CULTURAL INFLUENCE: Cöln was known for its rich cultural heritage, including art, music, and education. The environment would influence the upbringing of Moses and his siblings, providing them exposure to various cultural and intellectual ideas.

5. EDUCATION: EDUCATION would have been an important aspect of family life, with emphasis placed on both religious education and secular subjects. As the eldest brother, Moses might have started formal schooling, laying the foundation for his future education.

CONCLUSION

In summary, Moses Hess's experience as an older brother when Samuel was born in 1817 would have been shaped by family dynamics, a nurturing environment, and the socio-political context of post-Napoleonic Cöln. These early experiences would contribute to his identity and familial relationships as he navigated the complexities of childhood during a period of significant change and development in Germany.

MOSES "MAURICE" HESS was 13 years old when his mother, Eva Scheva Susmann Seltzer, passed away in Bonn in 1840. This loss would have had a profound impact on him and his family, influencing both their personal lives and the family dynamics. Here's an overview of the circumstances surrounding this event and its broader context:

Family Dynamics and Impact of Loss

1. Emotional Impact: The death of a mother during adolescence is a significant event that can lead to a range of emotions, including grief, confusion, and a sense of loss of guidance. At 13, Moses would be in a formative stage of his life, dealing with the complexities of adolescence and now facing the challenge of navigating this period without his mother.

2. FAMILY STRUCTURE: With the loss of Eva, the family dynamic would have shifted considerably. David, as the father, would need to take on both parental roles, which could lead to increased responsibilities for Moses and his siblings. Moses might have felt compelled to help support the family emotionally and practically during this difficult time.

3. SIBLINGS' RELATIONSHIP: The bond between Moses and his brothers, Lazarus and Samuel, could have strengthened in the wake of their mother's passing as they leaned on each other for support. They may have needed to provide emotional support to one another, sharing their feelings of grief and helping to fill the void left by their mother.

BROADER CONTEXT IN Bonn (1840)

1. Health Conditions: During the early 19th century, many diseases and health conditions were prevalent due to limited medical knowledge and healthcare resources. The loss of mothers during childbirth or due to other health issues was common, and communities often faced high mortality rates.

2. JEWISH COMMUNITY: In 1840, the Jewish community in Bonn was likely dealing with its own set of challenges, including social and legal restrictions. The community provided support for grieving families, often through communal rituals and mourning practices.

---

3. CULTURAL AND SOCIAL Life: The early 1840s were a time of cultural richness in Germany. The Romantic movement influenced art, literature, and music, which could have offered Moses a means of coping with his grief through creative expression or engagement with the arts.

---

4. POLITICAL CLIMATE: The period was marked by growing calls for political reform and Jewish emancipation. The experiences of Jewish families, including the Hess family, would be influenced by broader movements advocating for rights and social change, impacting their daily lives and future opportunities.

CONCLUSION

Moses's experience of losing his mother at the age of 13 would have been a pivotal moment in his life, shaping his emotional landscape and his relationships with his family. The broader context of Bonn during this time, including the social, cultural, and political environment, would have also influenced how he and his family coped with this significant loss, ultimately impacting Moses's path as he transitioned into adulthood.

WHEN MOSES "MAURICE" Hess was 13 years old, in 1826, matches were invented. The introduction of matches marked a significant advancement in technology and everyday life. Here's an overview of what this development meant during that time, along with its potential impact on Moses and his family:

Context of Match Invention (1826)

1. Historical Significance: The invention of the friction match is credited to John Walker, an English chemist, who created the first modern match that could ignite through friction. This innovation greatly simplified the process of starting fires compared to the more labor-intensive methods used previously, such as flint and steel or tinder.

2. IMPACT ON DAILY Life:

Convenience: Matches made it much easier for households to light fires for cooking, heating, and lighting. This convenience would have been particularly significant for a family like the Hess family, who would rely on fire for many aspects of daily living.

Safety: While matches were easier to use, they also posed new safety concerns. Fire accidents could become more common if children played with matches, which may have been a worry for parents.

3. CHANGES IN HOUSEHOLD Practices: With the availability of matches, the way households managed fire would have changed. Families could more easily light candles or stoves, leading to a greater reliance on these conveniences for light and warmth.

BROADER CONTEXT IN Bonn (1826)

1. Economic and Social Changes: The mid-1820s were a time of social and economic transformation in Europe, particularly following the Napoleonic Wars. Innovations like matches were part of a broader trend toward industrialization and modernization, impacting various aspects of life, including commerce and industry.

---

2. CULTURAL SHIFTS: The increased convenience of lighting fires with matches could also have implications for social and cultural gatherings. People could gather more comfortably in homes that were easier to heat and illuminate, fostering community connections.

---

3. EDUCATIONAL CONTEXT: As Moses was entering his teenage years, the invention of matches may have coincided with changes in education. With more accessible fire, studying at home would become easier, allowing for longer study hours during the evenings.

CONCLUSION

In summary, when Moses Hess was 13 years old and matches were invented in 1826, it represented a turning point in everyday life, affecting household practices, safety concerns, and social interactions. This technological advancement would have influenced not only the Hess family's day-to-day activities but also the broader societal context in Bonn, marking a period of change and adaptation. Moses would have been growing up in a world increasingly shaped by innovation, which would lay the foundation for his future experiences and opportunities.

MOSES "MAURICE" HESS was 26 years old in 1839 when photography became publicly available, thanks to the pioneering work of Louis Daguerre and his invention of the daguerreotype. This period marked a significant shift in how people captured and viewed images. Here's an overview of the implications of this technological advancement for Moses and the broader context of society at that time:

Impact of Photography on Society (1839)

1. Cultural Shift: The advent of photography transformed the way people perceived themselves and their world. It allowed for more accurate representations of people, places, and events. The ability to capture images would eventually become integral to personal and social identity.

2. ACCESSIBILITY AND Demand: Initially, photography was primarily a luxury for the wealthy due to the costs involved in equipment and processing. However, as the technology advanced and became more accessible, it started to appeal to a wider audience. This democratization of image-making would have begun to influence how ordinary families, including the Hess family, documented their lives.

3. PORTRAITURE AND Family Records: For families, the ability to have portraits taken became a way to commemorate significant life events, such as marriages, births, and deaths. Moses, now a young adult, might have considered capturing his own portrait or that of his growing family, including his wife and children.

4. INFLUENCE ON MEMORY and History: Photography changed how people remembered their past and how history was recorded. Instead of relying solely on written descriptions or paintings, individuals could now keep visual records of their lives, creating a more tangible connection to their memories.

BROADER CONTEXT IN Bonn and Germany (1839)

1. Political Climate: In 1839, Europe was experiencing a wave of political unrest and calls for reform. The 1848 revolutions were on the horizon, and photography could serve as a tool for political movements, documenting protests and social changes.

---

2. JEWISH IDENTITY: For the Jewish community, the ability to capture images could also play a role in shaping communal identity and visibility in a society where they often faced discrimination. Photographs could help assert their presence and participation in broader cultural narratives.

---

3. ARTISTIC DEVELOPMENTS: The rise of photography also influenced the art world, leading to new discussions about representation, realism, and the role of the artist. As an aspiring intellectual or artist, Moses may have engaged with these new ideas, reflecting on how photography changed perceptions of art and beauty.

CONCLUSION

When Moses Hess turned 26 and photography became publicly available in 1839, it marked the beginning of a new era in visual culture. This technological advancement would profoundly impact family dynamics, social identity, and historical documentation. Moses, navigating his young adulthood, would witness and perhaps partake in the societal shifts brought about by this innovation, influencing how he viewed his own life and legacy. The ability to capture moments through photography would resonate deeply with the themes of memory and history that would later influence his own work and the legacy he aimed to leave behind.

MOSES MAURICE HESS was 33 years old in 1846 when the sewing machine was patented by Elias Howe in the United States, with similar developments by Isaac Singer and others soon after. The introduction of the sewing machine represented a transformative technological advancement, particularly in the textile and garment industries. Here's an overview of its significance and the broader context during that time:

Impact of the Sewing Machine on Society (1846)

1. Revolutionizing Textile Production:

Increased Efficiency: The sewing machine drastically increased the speed and efficiency of sewing compared to hand-stitching. This innovation allowed garments and textiles to be produced more quickly and with greater uniformity.

Mass Production: The sewing machine facilitated the rise of the ready-to-wear clothing industry. This change meant that clothing could be produced in larger quantities, making it more accessible and affordable for a broader segment of society.

---

2. INFLUENCE ON DOMESTIC Life:

Women's Work: Sewing machines changed domestic life, particularly for women. Many women who previously engaged in hand sewing at home found opportunities to work with sewing machines, leading to a new wave of employment in factories and dressmaking establishments. This shift offered some women a degree of financial independence.

Home Sewing: The sewing machine also allowed families to create their own clothing and textiles at home more efficiently. For the Hess family, this could mean producing clothing for themselves and their children more easily.

---

3. CULTURAL SHIFTS:

Fashion and Style: The availability of more affordable clothing led to greater experimentation with fashion and styles. Families could more easily keep up with changing trends, impacting social status and identity.

Creativity and Craftsmanship: While mass production increased, it also sparked discussions about craftsmanship versus industrial production. Some individuals may have begun to view sewing as a creative outlet, utilizing machines to enhance their designs.

BROADER CONTEXT IN Bonn and Germany (1846)

1. Industrialization: The mid-19th century marked a period of significant industrial growth in Europe, including Germany. The

sewing machine was part of this broader trend toward mechanization, which transformed many industries and altered labor practices.

---

2. JEWISH COMMUNITY and Economic Opportunities: For the Jewish community in Bonn, the sewing machine and industrialization could present new economic opportunities. Some families might have engaged in textile trades, taking advantage of advancements to improve their livelihoods.

---

3. POLITICAL CLIMATE: As Europe was on the brink of the revolutions of 1848, there was growing awareness and dissatisfaction with social inequalities. Economic changes brought about by innovations like the sewing machine could both empower individuals and highlight disparities between social classes.

CONCLUSION

In 1846, when Moses Hess was 33 years old and the sewing machine was patented, this innovation represented a significant turning point in domestic life, labor, and the textile industry. The increased efficiency of garment production would have impacted Moses and his family, both economically and socially. As someone living during a time of rapid change, Moses would witness how these technological advancements influenced societal structures, family dynamics, and the broader context of Jewish life in Bonn and beyond. The sewing machine symbolized not only a practical tool for everyday life but also a catalyst for broader cultural shifts in the 19th century.

WHEN MOSES MAURICE Hess was 39 years old, his father, Nathan David Hess, passed away in 1851. This period in Moses's life was significant for several reasons, particularly as it marked the loss of a parental figure and was set against a backdrop of social, political, and technological changes in Europe. Here's an overview of the implications of this event and the context surrounding it:

Personal Impact of Nathan David Hess's Death

1. Emotional Loss: The death of a parent is often a profound emotional event. Moses would have faced grief, reflecting on his relationship with his father and the values and teachings he imparted. Nathan's passing may have prompted Moses to consider his legacy and the responsibilities he now held as a father himself.

2. FAMILY DYNAMICS: Moses had already experienced the loss of his mother when he was 13. The death of Nathan would have further altered the family structure, potentially placing greater responsibility on Moses to support and guide his siblings and his own children during this time of transition.

3. INHERITANCE AND Legacy: Following Nathan's death, there may have been discussions regarding inheritance and family obligations. This could include financial responsibilities or the continuation of family traditions, particularly within the Jewish community.

BROADER CONTEXT IN 1851

1. Industrialization and Modernization: The mid-19th century was marked by rapid industrialization across Europe. In Germany, cities like Bonn were experiencing significant changes in economic structures and labor. As a businessman, Moses might have been affected by these shifts, which would have influenced his family's financial situation and opportunities.

2. CULTURAL SHIFTS: The impact of Enlightenment ideas continued to shape society, affecting cultural practices, including those within the Jewish community. The period was marked by increasing discussions around secularism, identity, and the role of Jews in European society, which could have influenced Moses's own beliefs and aspirations.

3. POLITICAL CLIMATE: The revolutions of 1848 had brought about significant political change in Europe, including calls for greater rights and representation. By 1851, while the immediate revolutionary fervor had subsided, the political landscape was still in flux. For Moses, as a Jewish man in Germany, these changes may have created both opportunities and challenges regarding his status and rights within society.

TECHNOLOGICAL ADVANCEMENTS

1. Photography: The previous decade had seen the introduction of photography, which would have begun to affect how families documented their lives. Moses may have started to engage with this new medium, capturing memories of his own family as he navigated life as a father and a community member.

2. SEWING MACHINES: With the advent of sewing machines a few years earlier, the textile industry was undergoing significant transformation. This innovation could have impacted Moses's economic ventures, particularly if he or his family were involved in textile production or clothing retail.

CONCLUSION

Moses Hess, at 39 years old in 1851, faced a pivotal moment with the death of his father, Nathan David Hess. This personal loss intersected with a time of great change in Germany, characterized by industrialization, shifting cultural norms, and evolving political landscapes. As he navigated his responsibilities as a father and son, Moses would have also been influenced by the broader societal transformations occurring around him, shaping his worldview and legacy in profound ways. The loss of his father might have prompted him to reflect on his own identity and the future he envisioned for his children in a rapidly changing world.

Samuel Hess[3]

In 1817, when Samuel Hess was born in Cöln (now Cologne), Germany, Europe was emerging from the upheaval of the Napoleonic Wars, and society was just beginning to stabilize. The birth of Samuel coincided with a time of innovation, with the invention of the bicycle that year being a symbol of creativity and progress, while other notable changes were shaping daily life.

Social and Economic Context

1. Post-Napoleonic Era:

Restructuring and Recovery: Following Napoleon's defeat in 1815, Europe was reshaped by the Congress of Vienna, which sought to restore order and stabilize political boundaries. In German territories, including the Rhineland where Cöln was located, the Prussian influence was increasing, bringing about changes in governance, law, and daily administration.

Economic Challenges: Many regions in Europe, including Germany, were struggling with economic hardships. The war had disrupted trade and agriculture, and the recovery was slow. While towns and cities began to revitalize, rural areas faced poverty, and many families relied on subsistence farming or small trades.

2. INDUSTRIAL BEGINNINGS:

The early 19th century marked the start of industrialization in Europe, though it was more gradual in Germany compared to England.

Innovations were beginning to affect agriculture and textile production, creating a shift in labor and the beginning of an urban migration pattern as people moved to cities for work.

New Inventions: While machinery was still limited in German towns, 1817 saw a creative milestone with Karl Drais's invention of the "Draisine," also known as the "running machine" or the "hobby horse"—an early version of the bicycle. It allowed people to travel more efficiently and symbolized the ingenuity emerging in Europe, though it was primarily available to the wealthy or curious.

Life in Cöln (Cologne)

1. Religious and Cultural Life:

Jewish Community: For Jewish families like the Hess family, life in Cöln would have been shaped by tight-knit community bonds. The Jewish population faced restrictions on residence, profession, and movement, but communities remained resilient and resourceful. Jewish families often focused on commerce, trade, and craftsmanship, contributing to the local economy.

Cultural Vibrancy: Cöln was a vibrant city with historical ties dating back to the Roman Empire, and its position on the Rhine River made it a center of trade. Markets and festivals were common, providing a sense of liveliness and community gathering.

2. DAILY LIFE AND OCCUPATIONS:

Craftsmanship and Commerce: Many German towns, including Cöln, had strong artisanal traditions, where trades like shoemaking, tailoring, and carpentry were common. In some cases, entire families might work together in these trades. Economic opportunities in Cöln were modest, and while the city was still a few decades from full industrialization, it was gradually modernizing.

Agriculture and Markets: While Cöln was an urban area, the surrounding regions were agricultural, with farms supplying food and goods to the city. Markets were central to daily life, and families often traded and sold their products there.

3. POLITICAL CLIMATE:

Prussian Rule: With the Rhineland now under Prussian control, the local population was adjusting to Prussian governance, which included stricter laws and a new administrative system. For Jewish families, this could mean both opportunities and restrictions, as Prussia had a complex relationship with Jewish rights. While some Jewish communities gained more rights over time, others faced limitations on property ownership and professional licenses.

Broader Trends and Innovations

1. Scientific Curiosity and Innovation:

The invention of the "running machine" or early bicycle by Karl Drais showcased an era of innovation in personal transportation. Although it wasn't yet widely accessible, it symbolized humanity's drive for discovery and technology, hinting at a future where inventions would transform daily life.

2. INTELLECTUAL CLIMATE:

The intellectual movement of Romanticism was gaining popularity, emphasizing individual experience, nature, and emotion. This movement affected the arts, literature, and philosophy, and would influence many thinkers in Germany.

Conclusion

In 1817, the year Samuel Hess was born, Cöln was a city deeply rooted in tradition yet subtly shifting toward modernity. The early bicycle's invention represented a future-oriented spirit emerging amid the aftermath of the Napoleonic era. While life for most families, including the Hess family, was centered on trades, community, and traditional roles, they were also on the cusp of social and technological transformations that would reshape the 19th century. For Samuel, growing up in this period meant experiencing the first ripples of industrial change, while observing a society still grounded in customs, resilience, and the tight-knit bonds of family and faith.

AT THE AGE OF EIGHT, Samuel Hess faced a profound and formative loss with the passing of his mother in 1825. This would have been a deeply impactful event for a young child, shaping his early years in many ways.

Personal Impact of His Mother's Death

1. Emotional and Psychological Effects:

Grief and Adjustment: Losing a mother at such a young age would have been a challenging experience for Samuel. Without the emotional and nurturing presence of a mother, he may have struggled with feelings of loneliness and sadness. Family, especially siblings and extended relatives, would have likely played a significant role in supporting him during this time.

Role of Father and Family: With his father, David, now the primary caregiver, Samuel's relationship with him may have deepened. David would likely have had to take on new responsibilities to ensure the family's well-being and stability, possibly with the help of Samuel's older siblings.

______

2. RELIGIOUS AND CULTURAL Practices:

Mourning Traditions: In Jewish communities, mourning traditions like shivah (a seven-day mourning period) and yahrzeit (annual remembrance) would have offered structure and ritual around the loss. These practices might have provided Samuel a way to connect with his mother's memory and receive support from the community.

______

3. GROWING UP WITH a Sense of Responsibility:

In the absence of his mother, Samuel may have taken on additional responsibilities within the family as he grew older. In many families of that time, children contributed to household tasks, and this sense of responsibility would have been especially relevant for Samuel after his mother's death.

The Broader Context in 1825

1. Social Changes and Industrial Beginnings:

In the 1820s, German society was slowly transitioning toward industrialization, which affected urban life, including in cities like Cöln. While changes were gradual, new technologies and shifting economies were creating opportunities as well as uncertainties.

---

2. POLITICAL CLIMATE in Germany:

The political landscape in the German states was evolving, with increasing Prussian influence in the Rhineland where Cöln was located. Prussian governance brought a new legal system, which, while modernizing in some respects, maintained limitations for certain groups, including Jews. The Hess family would have been aware of these challenges, and the loss of a mother would make the family's resilience and adaptability all the more essential.

---

3. TECHNOLOGICAL AND Cultural Advancements:

The early 19th century was a time of curiosity and scientific progress. Though many technological advances were yet to reach everyday life, the era's spirit of discovery was evident. Growing up during this period, Samuel would likely have seen the gradual introduction of inventions and new ways of thinking that would shape his adult life.

Conclusion

For young Samuel, his mother's passing in 1825 would have been a life-altering experience. This loss meant adjusting to life without her support while relying more on his father and siblings. In a time marked by gradual social and industrial changes, Samuel's family structure and the responsibilities he undertook would shape his resilience and identity as he matured in a period of both personal and societal transformation.

AT 21, SAMUEL HESS witnessed the public introduction of photography in 1839, a groundbreaking advancement that captured society's imagination and would ultimately change how people preserved memories and recorded events. The availability of photography would have been a significant cultural shift, as it was a new, more accessible way to capture reality and history.

Photography in 1839: A New Era of Visual Memory

1. Introduction of the Daguerreotype:

In 1839, Louis Daguerre's invention of the daguerreotype was presented to the public in France, quickly sparking widespread interest across Europe. The daguerreotype allowed for detailed, sharp images, unlike anything people had seen before. For the first time, people could capture accurate likenesses of themselves and loved ones, making it particularly appealing to those who valued family connections and heritage, like the Hess family.

---

2. IMPACT ON SOCIETY:

Portraiture and Memory: Photography democratized portraiture. Previously, only the wealthy could afford painted portraits, but photography opened up opportunities for people of varied social backgrounds to capture their likenesses. This would have been meaningful for Jewish families like the Hess family, as they could preserve images of family members, strengthening connections across generations.

Documenting History: Photography became a way to document and share historical events, news, and everyday life. For people like Samuel, photography's emergence represented a shift in how society valued and remembered events.

3. PHOTOGRAPHY'S SPREAD and Accessibility:

Although photography was initially costly and less accessible to the general public, studios began opening in major European cities, allowing people to have their photographs taken at an affordable rate. While Samuel may not have immediately had access to a portrait, he likely would have known people who saw it or even visited a studio if one opened nearby.

4. THE RISE OF VISUAL Culture:

Photography marked the beginning of a more visually driven culture, where images could now speak alongside words. Newspapers, journals, and other publications began to see the potential of photography for news and illustration, bringing a new richness to printed media. For Samuel, this meant that society was becoming more connected through shared imagery, an early precursor to the image-driven culture that would continue to grow.

Personal Relevance for Samuel Hess

As Samuel was becoming a young adult, photography likely resonated with him as it symbolized progress and the power to hold onto one's legacy. Coming from a family familiar with loss and change, Samuel may have felt the appeal of capturing life moments in a way that would allow future generations to know their ancestors' faces and personalities. Photography's arrival during this time could have deepened Samuel's appreciation for memory, both familial and historical, giving him a new way to think about legacy and remembrance.

Conclusion

For Samuel, the public availability of photography in 1839 represented more than just a technological novelty. It was a bridge between memory and modernity, opening doors to preserving his family's history and contributing to a new way of seeing the world. The ability to capture and share images would have appealed not only to his personal values but also to a collective sense of heritage and identity, which was especially meaningful to communities navigating the complexities of 19th-century life in Germany.

AT 34, SAMUEL EXPERIENCED the loss of his father, David, in 1851. This would have been a deeply significant event in his life, marking the end of an era and shifting his role within the family and possibly within the community.

The Personal Impact of His Father's Passing

1. Emotional Loss and Reflection:

Legacy and Influence: The passing of a father often prompts reflection on familial values, traditions, and personal identity. Samuel would likely have looked back on the wisdom, guidance, and life lessons his father imparted. David's life had spanned momentous historical events, from the Napoleonic Wars to the early days of industrialization, and he likely shared stories and insights from his own experiences.

Family Dynamics: As Samuel and his siblings lost their father, they may have drawn closer to one another, sharing memories and responsibilities. Samuel's role as one of the older sons would have made him a natural leader within the family, helping to provide support and guidance, especially to any younger siblings.

---

2. STEPPING INTO A New Role:

Head of the Family: In the absence of his father, Samuel likely assumed more responsibilities, both within his immediate family and potentially as a figure within the extended family. This could include managing family affairs, supporting younger relatives, or carrying forward family traditions and values.

Continuing Traditions: Given the importance of legacy within Jewish families of this time, Samuel may have felt a heightened sense of duty to honor his father's memory. This could have influenced how he raised his own children, with a focus on preserving cultural and religious values that his father had instilled.

The Broader Context in 1851: A Time of Change

1. Economic Shifts:

Industrialization was progressing rapidly in the 1850s, transforming the economy and bringing about new social structures. David's passing marked the end of a generation that had known pre-industrial ways of life. Samuel, coming into his own in this changing world, would have to navigate the challenges and opportunities of an industrializing Germany.

2. JEWISH EMANCIPATION and Community Life:

Throughout Germany, Jews were beginning to see greater legal rights and social opportunities, although there were still significant hurdles to equality. For Samuel, his father's passing may have highlighted how much had changed over the years and what challenges remained. If David had been involved in the Jewish community, Samuel might have felt a duty to continue his father's work, supporting family and community cohesion during a period of social transformation.

3. TECHNOLOGICAL ADVANCEMENTS:

The world Samuel lived in was more connected and innovative than the one his father had been born into. Photography was now becoming more accessible, the telegraph had made long-distance communication much faster, and industries were expanding. Samuel, navigating these changes without his father's guidance, would have had to adapt and perhaps become a source of guidance himself for younger generations on how to thrive in this new, rapidly evolving society.

Concluding Reflections

The loss of his father in 1851 would have marked a period of profound change and growth for Samuel. He was now tasked with preserving his father's legacy and continuing the family's values in an era marked by progress, industrialization, and shifting societal norms. David's passing may have left Samuel with a stronger sense of purpose to honor his family's past while stepping confidently into a world that looked vastly different from the one his father had known. This transitional period likely deepened Samuel's resilience, shaping his identity as both a family leader and a bridge between generations.

Heinrich Rophinski[4]

When Heinrich Rophinski was born in Germany in 1851, the country was in the midst of social and political transformations, caught between the old order and the rumblings of change. Here's a look at what life was like at that time, especially for a family with only one parent listed:

Social and Political Context

1. Fragmented Germany:

In 1851, "Germany" was not yet a unified nation. Instead, it was a collection of 39 independent states and principalities in the German Confederation, which had been established after the fall of the Holy Roman Empire in 1815. This fragmentation meant that political policies and living conditions varied greatly depending on the region.

The revolutionary uprisings of 1848–49, which had called for unification and democratic reforms, had recently been suppressed. Reactionary forces had regained control, and there was a conservative pushback, leading to a period of political repression and a delay in unification efforts. However, these revolutionary ideals planted seeds for future changes in German society.

2. SOCIAL CLASS AND Family Dynamics:

For children born out of wedlock or with only one listed parent, like Heinrich, life could be especially challenging. Social norms were still very traditional, and illegitimacy could carry significant stigma. Single mothers often faced economic hardship and societal judgment, making it difficult for them to support their children alone.

If Anna Elizabet was indeed raising Heinrich by herself, she might have worked as a domestic servant, seamstress, or factory laborer, roles that were commonly available to women but poorly paid. Such jobs would demand long hours and offer little security, so she would likely have faced many difficulties providing for her son.

---

3. RURAL LIFE AND URBANIZATION:

Many Germans still lived in rural areas in 1851, with agriculture being the main source of employment. However, urbanization was accelerating, and people were increasingly moving to cities seeking work in factories, especially in regions like the Rhineland and Prussia.

Life in urban centers could be harsh. Cities were overcrowded, and sanitation was poor, leading to frequent outbreaks of disease. This urban migration began to expose rural populations to new, industrialized lifestyles, though for the poorer classes, this often meant low-paying jobs and inadequate housing.

Economic Landscape

1. Industrial Growth:

Germany's industrialization was underway, particularly in mining, ironworks, and textiles, though it was uneven across the confederation. This growing industrial base was starting to reshape the economy, moving away from agrarian dependency toward a modern industrial society. By the 1850s, Germany was on the path to becoming a major industrial power, but economic benefits were not equally distributed.

For the working class, economic stability remained elusive, and child labor was common, as families needed every member to contribute to the household income. This reality might have affected Heinrich's childhood as he grew older, particularly if he and his mother were struggling financially.

2. AGRICULTURAL HARDSHIPS:

Agriculture was still essential to the German economy, but the shift to industrial jobs was disrupting traditional farming life. Economic pressures in agriculture, including low prices for crops and competition with industrial wages, were pushing many small farmers and laborers to cities, intensifying urban poverty.

The price of bread and other essentials was often high, creating a constant struggle for poor families to afford basic needs. Food insecurity and malnutrition were realities for many Germans, especially those living in rural or low-income urban areas.

Living Conditions and Health

1. Health and Disease:

In 1851, Germany had limited medical knowledge and infrastructure, which meant that diseases like cholera, tuberculosis, and typhus were common and often fatal, especially in crowded, unsanitary city areas.

Without modern sanitation or access to healthcare, many families faced the constant risk of illness. Child mortality was high, and the absence of a father figure could further strain a household's ability to care for its children.

---

2. HOUSING AND BASIC Amenities:

Housing was modest for most Germans, often lacking adequate space, light, and ventilation. Urban families commonly lived in cramped, multi-family buildings, while rural dwellers typically had small, humble homes.

Basic amenities, such as running water, plumbing, and heating, were often unavailable, particularly for the lower classes. People relied on shared wells, outdoor privies, and wood or coal stoves, making daily life a challenge.

Cultural and Social Norms

1. Religious Influence:

Religion played a central role in daily life, with both Catholicism and Protestantism being dominant. The church was not only a spiritual guide but often a social support system, offering aid to struggling families, particularly single mothers like Anna Elizabet.

In smaller communities, local churches provided social networks that were essential for survival. If Anna Elizabet was connected to a supportive religious community, it could have helped alleviate some hardships associated with single parenthood.

2. EDUCATION:

The 19th century saw a growing emphasis on education, but schooling was often limited, especially for children from low-income families. Schooling was increasingly promoted, with some states introducing compulsory education in the 19th century, but financial hardships meant that children often worked rather than attended school.

Heinrich's educational prospects would likely have been limited by his family's socioeconomic position, although basic schooling might have been available in some areas, depending on regional policies and resources.

Conclusion

Heinrich Rophinski's birth in 1851 placed him in a society at the cusp of dramatic social, economic, and industrial change. His mother, Anna Elizabet, may have faced significant social and financial challenges, especially given the stigma attached to single motherhood at the time. Life for a single-parent household would have required resilience, creativity, and reliance on whatever social networks were available. Despite the challenges, Heinrich's early years also coincided with the beginning of Germany's transformation into a modern state, setting the stage for a new era that would offer both opportunities and challenges for his generation.

WITH HEINRICH ROPHINSKI'S passing on December 20, 1851, just months after his birth, his mother, Anna Elizabet, would have faced a particularly painful situation. Infant mortality rates in the mid-19th century were unfortunately high, partly due to the lack of advanced medical care, poor sanitation, and prevalent diseases, particularly among poorer families or those in crowded urban settings.

The winter season in Germany, when Heinrich passed, would have added challenges, as cold weather often exacerbated illnesses and limited access to fresh food and fuel for heating. Moreover, Anna Elizabet's grief would likely have been compounded by limited support options for a single mother. Though communities and religious organizations often provided some aid, mourning and recovery largely remained an individual and family matter.

Anna Elizabet (Unknown) Rophinski[5]

Anna Elizabet's life at the time of Heinrich's birth in 1851 would have reflected the challenging realities of a single mother in mid-19th century Germany, a time when societal expectations, limited economic opportunities, and the demands of raising a child largely on her own would have shaped her daily existence.

Social Standing and Stigma

As a single mother with only her name listed on Heinrich's records, Anna likely faced social stigma. In Germany at this time, single motherhood was not socially accepted, especially in more conservative communities. Legally and socially, women were still largely dependent on men, and any deviation from the norm could lead to alienation or judgment. This stigma would often limit her support network, impacting the aid she might receive from her community, extended family, or local institutions.

Economic Hardships

Without a husband, Anna's economic stability would have depended heavily on her own labor or any support she might secure from family or community. Single mothers in the 19th century often had limited options and were generally confined to lower-paying, labor-intensive jobs. Common occupations for women in her position included:

Domestic Work: Many women worked as maids or housekeepers, often residing in the homes of their employers and working long hours with few personal freedoms.

Factory Work: By the mid-1800s, Germany was beginning to industrialize, and factory jobs in textiles or small goods could provide some work, though conditions were difficult and pay was minimal.

Needlework or Seamstress Roles: Many women turned to sewing or mending garments, working from home if possible. This allowed her to care for Heinrich, but the income would likely be unreliable and low.

WITH THE ABSENCE OF social welfare programs, Anna's earnings would have been just enough to afford basics, and any illness or unexpected expense could quickly lead to financial instability.

Housing and Daily Living Conditions

Anna and Heinrich's living conditions would likely have been modest, possibly in a small, cramped apartment if they lived in a more urban area, or a simple cottage if they were in a rural village. Working-class homes of the time had basic furnishings and lacked modern amenities. Some challenges she may have faced included:

Heating and Cooking: Heat often came from a small stove, fueled by wood or coal. Keeping warm during winter could be costly, and she may have needed to conserve fuel to make it through the season.

Limited Sanitation: Most homes didn't have plumbing, and drinking water came from shared wells, often contaminated and a source of frequent illness.

Minimal Lighting: With limited access to candles or oil lamps due to cost, evenings were often dimly lit, making sewing or other evening tasks difficult.

HEALTH RISKS AND CHILDCARE

Infant and child mortality rates were high, especially among poorer families, and caring for a young child without access to healthcare would have been a constant worry for Anna. Common illnesses like measles, tuberculosis, or respiratory infections were frequent and often fatal in such unsanitary, cold environments.

Without support, childcare would have been a continuous challenge. If Anna worked outside the home, she might have needed to find someone to watch Heinrich, often relying on other working women, older children, or occasionally the charity of local women, though such help could be difficult to find.

Religion and Community

Religious institutions were a major part of daily life, often shaping values, expectations, and social assistance in 19th-century Germany. Many communities had strong ties to local churches, which could offer some support. For a single mother, the church might have been one of the few places to find solace or assistance, despite the accompanying stigma.

Anna might have attended services regularly, both as a source of spiritual support and to remain connected to her community. The church was also a place where she might seek some charitable aid, though assistance was often limited, inconsistent, and came with social judgment.

Emotional and Social Life

Emotionally, Anna's life would likely have been lonely and filled with worry. Single mothers were often isolated and focused heavily on survival, with little time or energy for social activities. Without a strong support network, Anna would have carried the burden of providing for and raising Heinrich largely on her own.

If she had supportive family members, they may have provided some comfort, but cultural expectations meant she was likely under significant pressure to be both mother and breadwinner. Any neighbors or friends who understood her position and provided help would have been invaluable in her life, even if simply to share the burden of daily hardships.

Final Thoughts

In summary, Anna's life as a single mother in 1851 Germany would have been marked by resilience in the face of considerable social and economic hardship. While industrialization and social changes were slowly advancing, the benefits were not yet widely felt by women in her position, leaving her dependent on her own resourcefulness and any limited support she could find. For women like Anna, raising a child was an act of determination and strength in a society that offered little support to those who stepped outside its norms.

WHEN HEINRICH ROPHINSKI passed away on December 20, 1851, the era in Germany was marked by significant social, economic, and political shifts, many of which influenced daily life, especially for lower-income families like Heinrich's.

Political Landscape and Change

Germany in 1851 was still a collection of independent states under the loose framework of the German Confederation, rather than a unified nation. The revolutions of 1848-1849, which had swept across Europe, including the German states, were fresh in memory. Although these revolutions ultimately failed to achieve lasting democratic reforms, they had instilled a sense of political consciousness and set the stage for future unification and reform.

The conservative monarchies had regained control, but public sentiment leaned towards change. Many people, especially in urban areas, were beginning to discuss ideas of national unity, social reforms, and personal freedoms. This political environment led to tensions and, for some, uncertainty about the future.

Industrialization and Economic Changes

Germany was on the cusp of industrialization. Railroads, factories, and new industries were beginning to reshape the economy, but the full effects of industrialization were still emerging. For lower-class families, economic life was still largely agrarian or based on small-scale local trades.

Work Opportunities: The rise of factories was opening up jobs in urban areas, but these jobs often involved long hours, low pay, and poor working conditions. Rural areas, where traditional agriculture remained dominant, faced economic challenges due to changes in farming practices and fluctuating food prices.

Migration to Cities: Many people from rural areas started moving to cities in search of work, resulting in crowded living conditions and poor sanitation in urban centers. It's possible Anna and Heinrich lived in such conditions if they were in a city, where the new industrial jobs could mean income but also harsh living conditions.

ADVANCES IN SCIENCE and Technology

While Germany was on the brink of a technological boom, the impact of innovations was just beginning to affect daily life. Some key developments around the time include:

Bicycles: The bicycle, invented in 1817, was gradually becoming a mode of transport, especially for the working class who needed affordable mobility.

Sewing Machines: Patented in 1846, sewing machines were slowly being introduced to workshops, which would later improve the textile industry and make clothing more accessible and affordable.

SOCIAL AND HEALTH CONDITIONS

Sanitation and healthcare in Germany were still rudimentary in 1851, especially in poorer neighborhoods. Water was often drawn from wells, and indoor plumbing was rare, leading to frequent outbreaks of diseases like cholera and typhoid in crowded areas. Infant mortality rates remained high, and diseases like tuberculosis, scarlet fever, and pneumonia claimed many lives, especially among the working class and poor.

For families like Anna's, who may not have had consistent medical care, infant deaths, unfortunately, were common. Heinrich's death at a young age might have been due to one of these illnesses, which were difficult to treat or prevent.

Religion and Community Life

Religion continued to play a central role in everyday life, influencing both social norms and community organization. The church often provided limited support for struggling families, although it could also be a source of moral judgment, particularly for single mothers. Nevertheless, for many, the church provided comfort, a sense of community, and occasional charity, especially in difficult times like the loss of a child.

Daily Life for Working-Class Families

The daily life of a working-class mother like Anna Elizabet would have been dominated by labor-intensive chores, economic hardship, and a strong sense of resilience. With limited support and social services, single mothers depended heavily on small networks of friends, extended family, or neighbors for any additional help. If she worked, she would have likely spent long hours away, potentially relying on friends or older children to help with childcare.

In Summary

Life in Germany at the time of Heinrich's death in 1851 was challenging, with the nation in a period of transition. The effects of recent revolutions, early industrialization, and scientific advancements were beginning to reshape society but had yet to alleviate the struggles of the working class. For Anna Elizabet, the death of her son may have been one of many hardships in a life marked by societal stigma, economic challenges, and limited support, yet she would have embodied the resilience typical of many single mothers of her era.

Johann Julius Riese[6]

JOHANN JULIUS RIESE'S birth and same-day baptism on June 5, 1851, in the Evangelische Kirche in Uhlstädt, Germany, reflects the traditions of the time for many Lutheran families. Born in the mid-19th century, Johann entered a Germany in the early phases of major social and economic transformations.

Religious Life

As a Lutheran family, Johann's parents likely held strong ties to their church community. Baptism was a sacred rite performed as early as possible, often the same day as birth, to ensure the child's spiritual protection. The Evangelische Kirche (Protestant Church) in Uhlstädt would have been central to community life, overseeing not only religious rites like baptisms, marriages, and funerals but also serving as a social hub. The church's involvement in the community often extended to providing guidance, basic education, and support in times of need.

Daily Life in Uhlstädt

In the rural region of Uhlstädt, life in 1851 would have been rooted in agriculture and traditional crafts. Many families worked as farmers, blacksmiths, weavers, and tailors, producing goods for local use and trade. Life was challenging and labor-intensive, with little automation. Most of the population depended on seasonal crops, and daily life was structured around the agricultural calendar. Families would have been large, with multiple generations often living together and working to support the household.

Social and Technological Changes

The early 1850s were marked by the aftereffects of the 1848 revolutions in Germany, which had introduced ideas of national unity and democratic reform, though the revolts themselves had not succeeded in unifying Germany. This period saw a shift in attitudes toward social reforms, education, and, increasingly, the role of the church in everyday life. Though largely rural, Uhlstädt would not have been entirely isolated from these ideas, and townspeople might have discussed the political shifts in Germany and the possibility of a united German state.

While Uhlstädt may not have experienced immediate industrial growth, advancements like the railroad, expanded in Germany during the 1840s and 1850s, would gradually bring greater access to markets, news, and goods. Over time, this would expose the community to urban centers and modern ideas.

Family and Community Bonds

In small communities like Uhlstädt, people relied heavily on each other for survival and mutual support. Family ties were paramount, and communities were tightly knit. For Johann, this meant growing up in a community where everyone knew each other, shared resources, and upheld social and religious values. This communal bond was often reinforced by the church, which was more than a religious institution—it was a cornerstone of identity and tradition.

In sum, Johann Julius Riese was born into a period of gradual transformation in Germany, yet his early life in Uhlstädt was likely marked by stability, traditional values, and a strong community centered around the Evangelische Kirche. His birth and baptism reflect the deep-rooted customs of his Lutheran heritage, shaping his early years in the village.

JOHANN JULIUS RIESE'S life was tragically brief, passing away just over two weeks after his birth on June 23, 1851. His parents, John Michael Riese and Hanne Rosine Mehlhorn, would have faced a challenging period following his death, especially in a close-knit, faith-centered community like Uhlstädt.

Life and Loss in 1851

Infant mortality was a sorrowfully common part of 19th-century life, and many families experienced the passing of young children due to illness or inadequate medical care. Communities like Uhlstädt would have witnessed these losses regularly, often bringing families closer together in grief and support. For John Michael and Hanne Rosine, the Evangelische Kirche likely provided both a place of mourning and a community that could offer comfort during their loss.

Religious Rites and Memorials

In accordance with Lutheran customs, Johann would have been given a small funeral service, often held within days of passing. The church would have overseen the burial, most likely in a local cemetery with other family members nearby. The ceremony would have been solemn and focused on faith, with scriptural readings and prayers emphasizing the hope of reuniting in the afterlife.

Moving Forward

In rural communities, loss was often a private burden, but shared grief strengthened communal bonds. For John Michael and Hanne Rosine, daily routines and hard work would have continued, perhaps intensifying the hope of future children. This difficult experience would shape them deeply, as families often commemorated lost children through records, memory, or other tributes within the home.

The short life of Johann Julius Riese, while brief, reflects the resilience of families in 19th-century rural Germany and the role of faith, family, and community in both celebrating and grieving life's fleeting moments.

Johann Michael Riese[7]

When Johann Michael Riese's son Friedrich Gottlieb Riese was born on August 6, 1849, Johann's life would have been shaped by various factors, including his role as a father, the socio-economic conditions of the time, and the broader historical context in which he lived. Here's a look at what Johann's life might have been like during this period:

Family Dynamics

1. Fatherhood: Johann would have been adjusting to his role as a father. With the birth of Friedrich, he would have felt a sense of responsibility and hope for his son's future. This was especially poignant given the recent loss of his infant son, Johann Julius, just weeks earlier. The joy of a new birth might have been tempered by the grief of his loss.

2. SUPPORT FROM FAMILY: In a rural German family, extended family often played a crucial role in daily life. Johann would have relied on his wife, Hanne Rosine, and possibly his parents or in-laws, for support with child-rearing and household responsibilities.

WORK AND ECONOMY

1. Agricultural Life: As a farmer or laborer, Johann's daily life would have revolved around agricultural work. In 1849, the harvest season would have been underway, and he would have been engaged in various farming activities, such as planting, tending to crops, and preparing for harvest.

2. ECONOMIC PRESSURES: The agricultural economy was subject to fluctuations, and Johann would have had to manage the challenges of crop yields, market prices, and the impacts of weather on farming. The transition from a feudal

system to more modern economic practices meant that Johann was likely navigating changing economic realities, which could add stress to family life.

SOCIAL AND POLITICAL Climate

1. Post-Revolutionary Atmosphere: Johann lived during a period of political unrest following the 1848 revolutions. While these changes were more pronounced in urban areas, rural communities were not entirely unaffected. Discussions around national identity, rights, and reforms may have influenced Johann's views, especially concerning his children's future.

---

2. COMMUNITY ENGAGEMENT: Johann's life would have been closely tied to his local community, with social interactions often centered around church and communal activities. The Lutheran Church would have played a vital role in community life, providing not only spiritual guidance but also a social network.

HEALTH AND MORTALITY

1. Concerns for Health: The mid-19th century was marked by high infant and maternal mortality rates. Johann would have been acutely aware of the fragility of life, especially following the loss of his son. The birth of Friedrich would have brought both joy and concern for his health and well-being.

---

2. LACK OF MEDICAL Resources: Access to medical care was limited in rural areas, and Johann would likely have relied on traditional remedies and the knowledge of local healers for any health issues. This situation would create a sense of urgency around family health, particularly for his wife during and after childbirth.

EMOTIONAL LANDSCAPE

1. Balancing Joy and Grief: The simultaneous experience of joy at the birth of Friedrich and sorrow from the loss of Johann Julius would have created a complex

emotional landscape for Johann. He might have felt a deep sense of love for his new son, tempered by the reality of loss and the desire to protect his family.

---

2. HOPE FOR THE FUTURE: Despite the challenges, Johann would have had hopes for Friedrich's future, envisioning opportunities for education and a better life. This hope might have been intertwined with aspirations for family stability and continuity in their farming way of life.

CONCLUSION

Johann Michael Riese's life when Friedrich was born in 1849 would have been a blend of personal and societal challenges. As a father navigating the complexities of grief and joy, he would have relied on his family, community, and faith to support him through the trials of rural life in mid-19th century Germany. The realities of farming, health concerns, and the changing political landscape would have shaped both his daily existence and his hopes for his son's future.

WHEN JOHANN JULIUS Riese was born on June 5, 1851, Johann Michael Riese would have experienced a range of emotions and circumstances that reflect the historical and personal context of the time. Here's an overview of what Johann's life may have been like during this period:

Family Dynamics

1. Fatherhood: The birth of Johann Julius would have brought Johann Michael immense joy and hope, especially following the earlier loss of his first son, Friedrich. He would likely have been eager to welcome his new child and see him grow. Being a father would have filled him with a sense of responsibility and commitment to provide for and protect his family.

---

2. SUPPORT FROM HANNE Rosine: Hanne Rosine, Johann's wife, would have played a critical role during this time. As a new mother, she would have faced the physical and emotional challenges of childbirth and the early days of caring for an

infant. The support of extended family, particularly female relatives, might have been essential in helping her through this period.

WORK AND ECONOMY

1. Agricultural Responsibilities: In 1851, Johann would have been deeply engaged in agricultural work. Depending on the season, he might have been involved in planting, tending to livestock, or preparing fields for harvest. Farming was labor-intensive, and managing a household with a newborn would have added to his workload.

---

2. ECONOMIC CHALLENGES: The economy in Germany during this period was evolving, with increasing industrialization starting to influence rural life. While Johann's primary livelihood would still rely on agriculture, he may have also been aware of changes in the local economy, including shifts in labor and market demands.

SOCIAL AND POLITICAL Climate

1. Post-Revolutionary Society: The aftermath of the 1848 revolutions was still influencing societal dynamics. Johann may have been aware of the broader discussions regarding rights, governance, and social reform. While rural areas might have felt less direct impact, there would still be a sense of change in the air.

---

2. COMMUNITY LIFE: Community ties would have been strong, and Johann likely participated in local events, gatherings, and church services. The Evangelische Kirche (Lutheran Church) would have been a central part of community life, providing spiritual guidance and social support.

HEALTH AND MORTALITY

1. Concerns about Health: The mid-19th century was marked by high infant and maternal mortality rates. Johann would have been acutely aware of the health risks

associated with childbirth, especially given his previous experience. He likely experienced anxiety about the well-being of both Hanne and their newborn son.

2. LIMITED MEDICAL Resources: Medical care was limited in rural areas, so Johann would have relied on traditional practices and local knowledge for any health issues. The reliance on family and community for support during illness or complications would have been crucial.

EMOTIONAL LANDSCAPE

1. Joy and Hope: The arrival of Johann Julius would have been a source of joy, bringing renewed hope for the family's future. Johann Michael might have dreamed of what his son would achieve, envisioning a life filled with opportunities and happiness.

2. LINGERING GRIEF: Despite the happiness of a new birth, Johann may still have felt the shadow of grief from the loss of his first son. This emotional complexity could have created a deeper appreciation for Johann Julius and a desire to protect him fiercely.

CONCLUSION

The birth of Johann Julius Riese in 1851 would have been a pivotal moment for Johann Michael Riese. As a father navigating the challenges of rural life, he would have been filled with both hope and concern. The responsibilities of farming, the realities of health care, and the strength of community ties would have shaped his daily life. In a time of transition and change, Johann Michael would have embraced fatherhood with love and dedication, cherishing the new life he welcomed into the world.

THE DEATH OF JOHANN Julius Riese on June 23, 1851, just 18 days after his birth, would have had a profound and multifaceted impact on his father, Johann

Michael Riese. Here's an exploration of how Johann Michael may have been affected by the loss of his newborn son:

Emotional Impact

1. Profound Grief: The death of a child, especially one so young, would likely have plunged Johann Michael into deep sorrow and grief. He may have experienced feelings of hopelessness, emptiness, and a sense of unfairness at having lost his son before he could really know him.

2. PARENTAL GUILT: Johann Michael might have grappled with guilt, questioning whether there was something he could have done differently to prevent Johann Julius's death. This feeling of helplessness can be common among parents who lose a child.

3. ANXIETY AND FEAR: The loss could have intensified Johann Michael's anxiety about the health and well-being of his surviving children. He may have become more protective and cautious, fearing further loss.

SOCIAL DYNAMICS

1. Isolation: In the face of such a personal tragedy, Johann Michael might have felt isolated from friends and neighbors who did not understand the depth of his sorrow. Social gatherings could have become uncomfortable for him, and he might have withdrawn from community interactions.

2. COMMUNITY SUPPORT: Conversely, he might have received support from family and friends, who could have offered condolences and shared their own experiences of loss. The sense of community could have provided some comfort during a painful time.

RELIGIOUS AND SPIRITUAL Reflection

1. Seeking Solace in Faith: As a Lutheran, Johann Michael may have turned to his faith for comfort and understanding in the face of tragedy. The church community might have provided him with a space for mourning and reflection.

2. EXISTENTIAL QUESTIONS: The loss of a child often leads to deep existential questioning. Johann Michael may have wrestled with questions about life, death, and the nature of suffering, seeking answers in scripture or through discussions with his pastor.

FAMILY DYNAMICS

1. Strain on Marriage: The loss of Johann Julius might have created strain in Johann Michael's relationship with his wife, Hanne Rosine. Grief can manifest differently in individuals, and if they processed their loss in contrasting ways, it could lead to misunderstandings or tension between them.

2. FOCUS ON SURVIVING Children: Johann Michael may have channeled his grief into ensuring the well-being of his surviving son, Friedrich, and any future children. This could have manifested as increased attention or, conversely, overprotection.

LONG-TERM EFFECTS

1. Enduring Grief: The loss may have led to long-term grief that could resurface during significant life events, such as birthdays or anniversaries of Johann Julius's death. Johann Michael might have carried the memory of his son throughout his life.

2. INFLUENCE ON PARENTING: The experience of loss might have shaped Johann Michael's approach to parenting. He may have become more nurturing, empathetic, or even overly cautious with his remaining children, reflecting the fragility of life he had come to understand.

CONCLUSION

The death of Johann Julius Riese would have profoundly affected Johann Michael Riese, creating an emotional landscape filled with grief, guilt, and longing. As he navigated this loss, he would have faced both the challenges and comforts that family, faith, and community can provide. In a time and society where child mortality rates were high, Johann Michael's experience would have been one of shared sorrow, reflecting the universal pain of losing a child while highlighting the resilience required to carry on.

Johanne Rosine "Henne" (Melhorn) Riese[8]

Life in Germany during the early 19th century, particularly around the time when Johanne Rosine "Hanne" Mehlhorn was born in 1815, was marked by significant social, political, and economic changes. Here are some aspects of life during this period:

Political Landscape

1. Post-Napoleonic Era: Hanne was born just after the end of the Napoleonic Wars (1803-1815), which had a significant impact on Germany. The Congress of Vienna in 1815 reshaped the map of Europe and established a balance of power, leading to the creation of the German Confederation, which included many independent states.

---

2. NATIONALISM AND Identity: The aftermath of the Napoleonic Wars fueled a sense of German nationalism. Many Germans began to advocate for unification, leading to a growing national identity that would eventually culminate in the formation of the German Empire in 1871.

ECONOMIC CONDITIONS

1. Agricultural Society: The economy in Germany during Hanne's early years was predominantly agrarian, with many people living in rural areas and working as farmers. Agriculture was the mainstay of the economy, and most families relied on subsistence farming.

---

2. EMERGENCE OF INDUSTRIALIZATION: Although Germany was still largely agrarian, the seeds of industrialization were beginning to take root. By the mid-19th century, cities like Cologne and others would start to see the growth of

factories, which would lead to increased urbanization and changes in the labor market.

SOCIAL LIFE AND CULTURE

1. Family Structure: Family was central to social life. Children were expected to help with household duties and work, especially in agricultural families. Women's roles were primarily centered around homemaking, child-rearing, and assisting with farm work.

2. RELIGIOUS LIFE: Germany was predominantly Christian, with a mix of Protestantism (especially Lutheranism) and Catholicism. Religious practices were integral to daily life, and church attendance was a common part of the community routine.

3. CULTURAL FLOURISHING: The early 19th century was also a time of cultural flourishing, with developments in music, literature, and philosophy. Figures like the Brothers Grimm were collecting folktales, and composers like Beethoven were shaping German music.

EDUCATION AND LITERACY

1. Limited Access to Education: Education was not universally accessible, especially for girls. While boys often received formal schooling, girls' education was typically focused on domestic skills. However, this period saw the beginnings of movements advocating for better education for women.

2. EMERGING LITERACY: Literacy rates were gradually increasing, particularly in urban areas, as more people began to see the value of education. This trend would continue to grow throughout the 19th century.

CONCLUSION

In summary, Hanne Mehlhorn's early life in Germany in 1815 would have been shaped by the lingering effects of the Napoleonic Wars, the transition towards industrialization, and the strong emphasis on family and community. While life was primarily agrarian and traditional, the era also set the stage for significant social and political changes that would define the later part of the century. The growth of national identity, the beginnings of industrialization, and the push for education would all play critical roles in shaping the lives of future generations in Germany.

WHEN JOHANNE ROSINE "Hanne" Mehlhorn was two years old in 1817, the invention of the bicycle marked a significant advancement in transportation technology. Here's an overview of life around that time, particularly with the context of the bicycle's invention and the social conditions of early 19th-century Germany:

The Bicycle's Invention

1. Early Development: The first bicycle, known as the "Draisine" or "running machine," was invented by Karl Drais in 1817. This early form of the bicycle was made of wood and did not have pedals; riders pushed themselves along with their feet. The invention was initially a curiosity and not widely adopted.

2. IMPACT ON TRANSPORTATION: Although the bicycle would not become popular until later in the 19th century, its introduction represented a shift towards personal mobility. It foreshadowed future developments in transportation, emphasizing individual mobility over reliance on horses and carriages.

LIFE IN GERMANY IN 1817

1. Agricultural Society: Most people in Germany continued to live in rural areas, relying on agriculture for their livelihood. Farms operated within a traditional structure, with families working together to manage crops and livestock.

2. RURAL AND URBAN Divide: While some cities were beginning to industrialize, most of the population still resided in the countryside. The pace of life in rural areas was slower, with seasonal rhythms dictated by farming cycles.

---

3. SOCIAL CHANGES: The early 19th century was a time of transition. The ideas of the Enlightenment were beginning to influence societal norms, leading to changes in how people thought about governance, individual rights, and education.

---

4. POLITICAL CONTEXT: The defeat of Napoleon in 1815 had created a new political landscape in Europe, including the formation of the German Confederation. Nationalism was growing, and many Germans began to think about unification and identity.

---

5. CULTURAL LIFE: THIS period saw a flourishing of culture, with increased interest in literature, music, and art. Figures like the Brothers Grimm were collecting folk tales, and the Romantic movement was gaining momentum in arts and letters, emphasizing emotion and individual experience.

---

6. FAMILY STRUCTURE and Gender Roles: Families were central to society, and traditional roles were prevalent. Women were often responsible for household duties, and children typically contributed to family work from a young age. Education for boys was more formal, while girls' education often focused on domestic skills.

CONCLUSION

At the time of the bicycle's invention, life in Germany was characterized by traditional agricultural practices, a slow transition towards industrialization, and a rich cultural environment. While the bicycle itself would take time to gain traction as a mode of transport, its invention was part of a broader narrative of innovation and change that would influence society in the decades to come. Hanne's early years would be filled with the rhythm of rural life and the gradual emergence of new ideas that would shape her world.

———————

WHEN JOHANNE ROSINE "Hanne" Mehlhorn was 11 years old in 1826, the invention of modern friction matches marked a significant technological advancement in daily life. Here's an overview of what life was like in Germany during this time, particularly considering the impact of match invention and the broader social context:

The Invention of Matches

1. Introduction of Friction Matches: In 1826, English chemist John Walker created the first modern friction match. These matches allowed for quick and easy ignition, revolutionizing how people could light fires for cooking, heating, and lighting. The convenience of matches gradually replaced more cumbersome methods, such as using flint and steel.

———————

2. ACCESSIBILITY AND Use: Initially, matches were not widely available or inexpensive. However, as production methods improved over the following decades, they became more accessible to the general public. This innovation significantly impacted everyday life, making it easier for families to start fires in their homes.

———————

LIFE IN GERMANY IN 1826

1. Agricultural Society: Germany remained predominantly agrarian, with many people engaged in farming and related occupations. Rural communities followed seasonal cycles, with work dictated by planting and harvesting times.

———————

2. SOCIAL STRUCTURE: Society was typically hierarchical, with a clear distinction between social classes. Landowners and wealthier farmers held significant power, while laborers and tenant farmers often struggled economically.

———————

3. POLITICAL CLIMATE: Following the Congress of Vienna in 1815, Europe experienced political changes, with various German states consolidating into the German Confederation. Nationalism was on the rise, and people began discussing ideas of unity and identity in anticipation of the eventual unification of Germany in the late 19th century.

------

4. CULTURAL DEVELOPMENTS: The early 19th century was a vibrant time for culture, particularly with the rise of Romanticism in literature, music, and art. German authors, poets, and musicians were celebrated figures, contributing to a growing national identity and pride.

------

5. EDUCATION AND LITERACY: Education was becoming more valued, particularly in urban areas. Boys were more likely to receive formal education, while girls were often educated at home, focusing on domestic skills. Literacy rates were gradually increasing, partly due to the spread of printed materials and public schooling.

------

6. RELIGIOUS LIFE: Germany was predominantly Christian, with a mix of Protestantism and Catholicism. Religious institutions played significant roles in community life, and church attendance was a regular part of social customs.

------

7. FAMILY DYNAMICS: Families remained central to social structure. Children were expected to contribute to household work from a young age. In rural areas, large families were common, as children were viewed as assets to help with farm labor.

CONCLUSION

At the time Hanne turned 11 in 1826, her world was influenced by the introduction of friction matches, which made everyday tasks more convenient. Life in Germany during this period was marked by an agrarian economy, social hierarchies, and emerging cultural movements. The changes occurring around her—both in terms of technology and societal norms—would shape Hanne's upbringing and the world she would continue to navigate as she grew older.

WHEN JOHANNE ROSINE "Hanne" Mehlhorn turned 24 in 1839, the advent of publicly available photography marked a significant cultural and technological shift. Here's an overview of life during that period in Germany, considering the impact of photography and the broader societal context:

The Introduction of Photography

1. Public Availability of Photography: In 1839, Louis Daguerre announced the daguerreotype process, making photography commercially viable for the first time. This innovation allowed people to capture images with unprecedented clarity, altering how individuals documented their lives and communities.

---

2. IMPACT ON SOCIETY: Photography began to change the way people perceived themselves and their surroundings. Portraits, landscapes, and scenes of daily life could now be captured and shared, leading to new forms of artistic expression and personal documentation.

---

3. ACCESSIBILITY: INITIALLY, photography was expensive and complex, limiting its use primarily to the wealthy or those willing to invest in the equipment and processes. However, over time, it would become more accessible to the broader public.

LIFE IN GERMANY IN 1839

1. Political Climate: The early 1830s in Germany were marked by a growing desire for political reform. The 1830 revolution in France inspired movements across Europe, including calls for greater democracy and national unity in the German states. This period laid the groundwork for future political changes, including the eventual unification of Germany in 1871.

---

2. SOCIAL CHANGES: The period saw the rise of the middle class, which was beginning to have more influence in society. Industrialization was starting to take root in some areas, leading to the growth of urban centers and shifts in labor patterns.

---

3. CULTURAL DEVELOPMENTS: The Romantic movement continued to flourish, emphasizing emotion, nature, and the individual's experience. Literature, music, and visual arts thrived, with figures like the Brothers Grimm and composers like Robert Schumann gaining recognition. The emergence of photography complemented these artistic trends by providing a new medium for expression.

---

4. EDUCATION AND LITERACY: The emphasis on education was increasing, with literacy rates gradually improving, especially in urban areas. Public education was becoming more widespread, and the value of literacy for social mobility and personal development was increasingly recognized.

---

5. FAMILY STRUCTURE: Family dynamics in Hanne's time were still traditional, with clear roles for men and women. While women primarily managed the household, their roles were evolving slightly due to the rising middle class and the changes brought about by industrialization. Children were expected to contribute to family work and education.

---

6. RELIGIOUS INFLUENCE: Religion continued to play a significant role in daily life. Protestantism was prominent in northern Germany, while Catholicism was more common in the south. Church attendance and religious festivals were important aspects of community life.

CONCLUSION

At 24 years old in 1839, Hanne Mehlhorn was witnessing a transformative period in history marked by the advent of photography, which would reshape personal and collective memories. The political and social landscape of Germany was changing, with increasing demands for reform and a burgeoning middle class. These developments would impact Hanne's experiences, as she navigated the complexities of life in an evolving society while witnessing the rise of new technologies that changed how people saw themselves and their world.

WHEN JOHANNE ROSINE "Hanne" Mehlhorn turned 31 in 1846, the invention of the sewing machine marked another significant technological advancement that would impact everyday life in Germany and beyond. Here's an overview of life during that time, focusing on the implications of the sewing machine and the broader social context:

The Invention of the Sewing Machine

1. Patent and Impact: In 1846, Elias Howe patented the first practical sewing machine, which revolutionized the textile industry and domestic sewing. This invention allowed for faster and more efficient production of clothing and textiles, significantly reducing the time and labor required for sewing tasks.

2. CHANGING HOUSEHOLD Dynamics: With the sewing machine, women could produce garments more quickly and with greater precision. This not only made clothing more affordable but also encouraged women to engage in sewing as a productive activity, potentially leading to a shift in their roles within the household.

3. COMMERCIALIZATION: The sewing machine facilitated the growth of ready-made clothing, transforming the fashion industry. Tailors and dressmakers could produce garments in larger quantities, leading to the rise of clothing shops and the commercialization of fashion.

LIFE IN GERMANY IN 1846

1. Political Climate: The political atmosphere in Germany was still marked by tensions and desires for reform. The Revolutions of 1848 were on the horizon, driven by widespread dissatisfaction with conservative governance and a demand for

national unity and democracy. Hanne would be witnessing increasing public discourse about rights and representation.

---

2. INDUSTRIAL REVOLUTION: Germany was in the early stages of industrialization, with factories beginning to emerge in urban areas. This transformation led to a shift from agrarian economies to more industrial-based economies, impacting labor patterns and urban migration.

---

3. SOCIAL CHANGES: As industrialization progressed, the traditional family structure began to evolve. Many families moved to cities for work, altering the dynamics of family life and creating new social classes, including a growing working class.

---

4. CULTURAL DEVELOPMENTS: The Romantic movement was still influential in literature, art, and music. The period saw continued growth in the arts, with figures like Franz Liszt and Richard Wagner making significant contributions. The rise of the middle class and increased literacy rates allowed more people to engage with cultural products.

---

5. EDUCATION AND WOMEN'S Roles: Education for women was gradually improving, with a growing emphasis on teaching girls skills such as reading, writing, and domestic arts, including sewing. While women's primary responsibilities still centered on the home, innovations like the sewing machine began to empower them economically and socially.

---

6. RELIGIOUS INFLUENCE: Religion remained an essential aspect of daily life in Germany, with the Protestant and Catholic communities playing significant roles in local governance and social norms. Festivals and community events often had religious undertones, reflecting the deep-rooted cultural importance of faith.

CONCLUSION

At 31 years old in 1846, Hanne Mehlhorn experienced a period of profound change driven by technological advancements, particularly the sewing machine, which transformed domestic and industrial sewing practices. As Germany approached a time of political upheaval and social transformation, Hanne was likely navigating the complexities of a changing society, where traditional roles were beginning to shift under the influence of industrialization and emerging ideas about women's rights and education. The combination of these elements contributed to a dynamic environment that would shape her life and the lives of those around her.

WHEN JOHANNE ROSINE "Hanne" Mehlhorn gave birth to her son, Friedrich Gottlieb Riese, on August 6, 1849, she was navigating a complex period in German history marked by significant social, political, and economic changes. Here's how these factors may have affected her:

1. Emotional and Psychological Impact

Motherhood and Responsibility: As a new mother, Hanne would have experienced a mix of joy and anxiety, common for women at that time. The responsibility of raising a child during a tumultuous period may have weighed heavily on her. She would likely be concerned about providing a stable environment for Friedrich amid political instability and health concerns.

Support Networks: In this era, family and community support were crucial for mothers. Hanne might have relied on her own mother, sisters, or neighbors for help with childcare and household duties, which would be vital given the challenges of childbirth and early motherhood.

2. SOCIAL AND ECONOMIC Context

Economic Changes: The Industrial Revolution was reshaping Germany's economy, leading to both opportunities and challenges. If Hanne's family was affected by industrialization, she might have felt the strain of economic fluctuations, which could impact her household's finances and resources available for raising a child.

Living Conditions: As urbanization progressed, living conditions in cities could be crowded and unhealthy. If Hanne lived in a burgeoning urban area, she would need to navigate potential public health issues, such as sanitation and access to clean water, which were significant concerns during this period.

---

3. POLITICAL CLIMATE

Revolutions of 1848-1849: The revolutionary atmosphere in Germany during this time could have influenced Hanne's life significantly. She may have been politically aware, feeling the effects of protests, strikes, and demands for social reform. These events might have shaped her views on motherhood and her aspirations for her child's future, particularly regarding education and political rights.

Impact of Conflict: The uncertainties of the revolution could also cause anxiety for her family. Hanne might have worried about the potential for violence or instability affecting her home life or her husband's work.

---

4. CULTURAL INFLUENCES

Role of Women: Hanne lived during a period when women's roles were beginning to shift. As ideas about women's rights and education were emerging, she might have been influenced by discussions in her community or church about women's contributions to society. This environment could have inspired her to seek opportunities for her son's education and well-being.

Cultural Enrichment: The Romantic movement's influence might have provided Hanne with access to literature, art, and music that emphasized family, nature, and emotion. These cultural elements could have provided her comfort and inspiration as she navigated her new role as a mother.

---

5. HEALTH CONSIDERATIONS

Maternal Health: Childbirth in the mid-19th century carried risks, and maternal mortality rates were higher than today. Hanne would have been aware of these dangers and may have been anxious about her health and recovery after childbirth.

Child Health: Infant mortality rates were also high during this period. Hanne would likely have felt a sense of vulnerability regarding Friedrich's health, motivating her to seek knowledge about childcare practices and potentially leading her to join support groups with other mothers.

CONCLUSION

Hanne's life as a 34-year-old mother in August 1849 was shaped by a confluence of personal and societal factors. The birth of Friedrich Gottlieb Riese marked a significant milestone, intertwining her emotional journey with the broader historical context of a nation in flux. The challenges of motherhood, economic conditions, political unrest, and cultural shifts would have deeply influenced her experience and the environment in which she raised her son. Hanne's aspirations for Friedrich's future and her approach to motherhood would likely reflect the complexities of the world around her.

WHEN JOHANNE ROSINE "Hanne" Mehlhorn gave birth to her son, Johann Julius Riese, on June 23, 1851, she was navigating a pivotal moment in both her personal life and the broader socio-political landscape of Germany. Here's an overview of what her life may have been like at that time:

1. Emotional and Psychological Impact

Experience of Motherhood: Having already given birth to Friedrich two years earlier, Hanne would have a mix of anticipation and experience. However, being a mother to two young children at the age of 36 might bring additional stress and exhaustion, particularly if she was managing a household with limited resources.

Fear and Anxiety: Given the high infant mortality rates during this time, Hanne may have felt anxious about Johann's health and survival. The emotional toll of worrying for her children's well-being would be significant, especially considering that her previous experiences with childbirth would inform her expectations.

---

2. HEALTH CONSIDERATIONS

Maternal Health Risks: At 36, Hanne was approaching an age where childbirth could carry higher risks. Complications during pregnancy and childbirth were not uncommon, so she may have felt anxious about her own health and recovery after giving birth.

Child Health: Johann Julius was born during a period when infant care knowledge was still rudimentary. Hanne likely relied on traditional practices and community knowledge for caring for her newborn while worrying about diseases that could affect infants.

---

3. SOCIAL AND ECONOMIC Context

Economic Conditions: The early 1850s in Germany were characterized by ongoing industrialization. If Hanne and her family lived in a town affected by these changes, they might have experienced both the benefits of economic opportunities and the challenges of urban life, including overcrowding and health hazards.

Living Conditions: Hanne's family might have faced difficulties in securing adequate housing, especially if the economic changes led to rising rents and increased demand for housing in urban areas.

---

4. POLITICAL CLIMATE

Post-Revolutionary Effects: Following the revolutions of 1848, Germany was in a period of political restructuring. Hanne may have been aware of the growing calls for reform and change, affecting her thoughts about her children's futures and the world they would grow up in.

Emerging National Identity: Hanne might have been influenced by the emerging sense of national identity in Germany, considering the potential implications for her sons as they grew older.

---

5. CULTURAL INFLUENCES

Education and Women's Rights: By 1851, discussions about women's education and rights were gaining traction in Germany. Hanne might have felt the effects of these changing societal norms and may have been motivated to ensure that her children received an education, especially Friedrich, who was nearing school age.

Cultural Climate: The influence of Romanticism and the burgeoning middle class meant that literature, music, and art played significant roles in daily life. Hanne could have found solace and inspiration in cultural activities, which were becoming more accessible to families of varying social standings.

---

6. COMMUNITY AND SUPPORT

Support Networks: The importance of community support would have been paramount. Hanne likely relied on family and neighbors for assistance, sharing the burden of childcare and household responsibilities with other mothers in her community.

Religious Life: Being part of a Lutheran community would have provided Hanne with spiritual support and a social network, which may have been a source of comfort and guidance during challenging times.

CONCLUSION

Johanne Rosine "Hanne" Mehlhorn's experience in June 1851 as a mother of two young children was shaped by various personal, social, and political factors. The birth of Johann Julius brought both joy and new challenges as she navigated motherhood, health concerns, and the changing landscape of her society. Hanne's aspirations for her children and her ability to manage the demands of family life during this transformative period would reflect her resilience and adaptability.

WHEN JOHANN JULIUS Riese passed away on June 23, 1851, at just 18 days old, the impact on his mother, Johanne Rosine "Hanne" Mehlhorn, would have been profound. Here are some specific aspects to consider regarding her emotional and social situation during this heartbreaking time:

Emotional Impact

1. Intense Grief: Losing a child so young would bring overwhelming sadness and despair. Hanne had only begun to bond with Johann, and his death would disrupt that early relationship.

2. SHORT-LIVED HOPE: The brief time between Johann's birth and death might have filled Hanne with a mix of joy and sorrow. The initial joy of bringing a new life into the world would have quickly turned to grief, intensifying her emotional turmoil.

3. LOSS OF FUTURE ASPIRATIONS: Hanne likely had hopes and dreams for her son, imagining milestones such as his first steps, first words, and future achievements. His death would abruptly cut off these possibilities, contributing to her sorrow.

SOCIAL CONTEXT

1. Isolation in Grief: While Hanne might have had support from family or friends, grief can often feel isolating. She may have found it difficult to share her feelings with others who may not fully understand the depth of her loss.

2. CULTURAL EXPECTATIONS: In 19th-century Germany, motherhood was highly valued. Losing a child could bring about feelings of shame or inadequacy, as societal norms often placed the onus on mothers for the health and survival of their children.

3. COMMUNITY RESPONSES: While there would have been community support during the mourning process, Hanne might also have faced societal pressure to move on quickly after Johann's passing. Grieving customs could vary, but she may have felt compelled to conceal her sorrow in public.

PHYSICAL HEALTH

1. Postpartum Recovery: Hanne would be recovering from childbirth, which itself could be physically taxing. The added emotional burden of grief could complicate her physical healing, impacting her overall well-being.

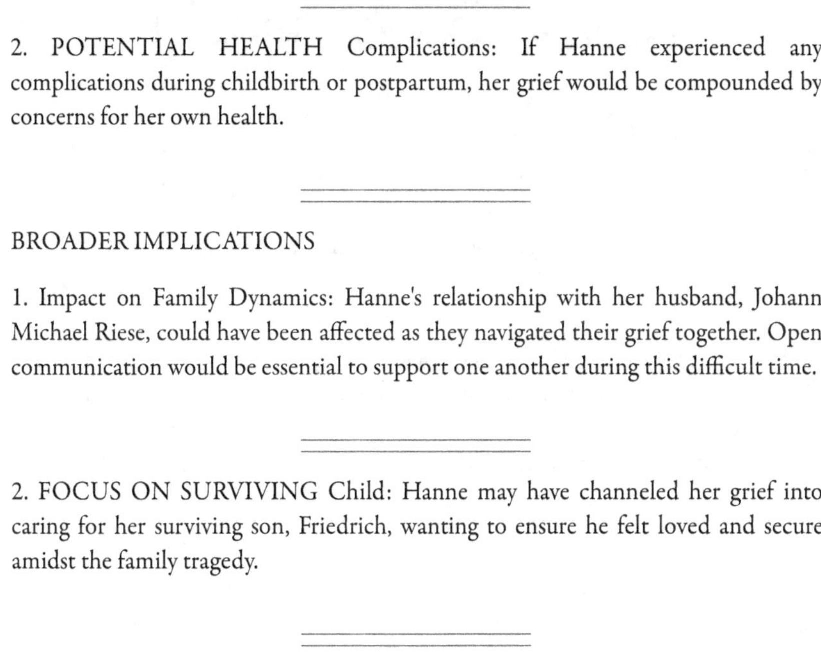

2. POTENTIAL HEALTH Complications: If Hanne experienced any complications during childbirth or postpartum, her grief would be compounded by concerns for her own health.

BROADER IMPLICATIONS

1. Impact on Family Dynamics: Hanne's relationship with her husband, Johann Michael Riese, could have been affected as they navigated their grief together. Open communication would be essential to support one another during this difficult time.

2. FOCUS ON SURVIVING Child: Hanne may have channeled her grief into caring for her surviving son, Friedrich, wanting to ensure he felt loved and secure amidst the family tragedy.

CONCLUSION

The death of Johann Julius Riese just 18 days after his birth would have been a devastating event for Hanne, affecting her emotional state, social interactions, and physical health. While she may have found some comfort in the support of family and community, the isolation and intensity of her grief would likely have left a lasting impact on her life and outlook as a mother. Balancing her grief while caring for her surviving child would become a central challenge during this period.

Frederich Gottlieb Riese[9]

Friedrich Gottlieb Riese was born on August 6, 1849, in Germany, during a time of significant social, political, and economic change. Here's an overview of what life was like in that era, particularly in the context of Friedrich's birth:

Historical Context

1. Post-Revolutionary Germany: Friedrich was born just after the revolutionary wave of 1848, when many Germans demanded national unity and democratic reforms. Though these uprisings ultimately failed to create a unified Germany, they spurred discussions about nationalism and rights that would resurface in later decades.

2. SOCIO-POLITICAL Climate: The late 1840s were marked by political unrest and a desire for change. There was an increasing push for more rights, education reforms, and an end to feudal practices. While rural communities like Uhlstädt may not have felt the full brunt of these changes immediately, the ideas were slowly permeating through society.

DAILY LIFE AND ECONOMY

1. Agricultural Society: Life in rural Germany during this time was largely agrarian. Most families were engaged in farming or related trades. The harvest season would have been crucial, and many families worked the land together. Friedrich's family would have depended on their crops for sustenance and income.

2. FAMILY STRUCTURE: Families were typically large, as many children were expected to contribute to the household's labor. Friedrich would likely have had siblings, including his recently deceased younger brother Johann Julius, which would have shaped the family dynamic and the support system around him.

RELIGIOUS INFLUENCE

1. Lutheran Traditions: As a Lutheran family, religious practices would have played a significant role in daily life. Baptisms, confirmations, and church attendance were important events that solidified family and community ties. The church would serve not just as a spiritual center but also as a community gathering place, especially during times of celebration or mourning.

2. EDUCATION: BY THIS time, some educational reforms were underway. While formal schooling was limited, there were efforts to improve literacy and education, often provided by the church. Friedrich may have attended a local school, learning basic reading and writing skills.

CHALLENGES

1. Health and Mortality: The mid-19th century saw high infant and maternal mortality rates. While Friedrich survived, his family had already faced the tragic loss of Johann Julius, a reminder of the fragility of life during this period. Diseases such as cholera and tuberculosis were prevalent, and access to medical care was limited.

2. ECONOMIC HARDSHIPS: The economy was primarily based on agriculture, and families often faced hardships due to poor harvests or changing market demands. The transition from a feudal system to more modern economic practices was just beginning, and rural areas often lagged behind urban centers in these developments.

CONCLUSION

Friedrich Gottlieb Riese's birth in 1849 marked the beginning of his life in a time of change and challenge. Growing up in a rural German community, he would have experienced the influences of his family's Lutheran faith, the realities of agricultural life, and the evolving socio-political landscape of the time. His family's recent loss and the broader context of societal shifts would shape his early experiences, embedding a sense of resilience and community support that characterized life in 19th-century Germany.

―――――――――――

WHEN FRIEDRICH GOTTLIEB Riese was just one year old and his younger brother Johann Julius was born and died within such a short span, it would have created a complex and challenging emotional landscape for the family, especially for their mother, Johanne Rosine "Hanne" Mehlhorn. Here are some considerations regarding the situation during that time:

Emotional Impact on Hanne

1. Overwhelming Grief: The loss of Johann would be particularly devastating for Hanne, especially so soon after his birth. With Friedrich still in his infancy, she would need to navigate her grief while also caring for him.

―――――――――――

2. FOCUS ON FRIEDRICH: Hanne might have felt compelled to focus her energy and affection on Friedrich during this period, seeking to maintain a sense of normalcy and security for him despite her profound sorrow.

―――――――――――

3. COMPLEXITY OF MATERNAL Instincts: As a new mother, Hanne would likely experience a mix of emotions, from joy in caring for Friedrich to despair over Johann's brief life. This duality could create internal conflict as she tried to manage her feelings.

―――――――――――

IMPACT ON FRIEDRICH

1. Lack of Understanding: At just one year old, Friedrich would not comprehend the loss of his brother. However, the atmosphere of grief in the home could affect him. Babies and young children often pick up on emotional cues from their parents and caregivers.

―――――――――――

2. MOTHER'S ATTENTION: With Hanne grieving, Friedrich might have sensed a change in his mother's attention and emotional availability. This could impact his early attachment and sense of security.

3. FUTURE FAMILY DYNAMICS: The loss of Johann could shape the family dynamics as Friedrich grew older. If Hanne's grief influenced her parenting style, it could impact Friedrich's development and his relationship with his mother.

SOCIAL CONTEXT

1. Community Support: The community may have rallied around Hanne and her family during this time of loss. Neighbors, friends, and extended family might have provided support, bringing food or offering assistance to help care for Friedrich.

2. CULTURAL MOURNING Practices: In 19th-century Germany, specific mourning customs and rituals were observed, which might have included wearing mourning clothing or observing a period of seclusion. Hanne might have felt pressure to conform to these customs while also caring for an infant.

FAMILY DYNAMICS

1. Father's Role: Johann Michael Riese, Hanne's husband, would also have been affected by the loss. His ability to provide support to Hanne and care for Friedrich would depend on his own grieving process and available resources.

2. STRENGTHENING BONDS: The shared experience of loss could either strengthen the bond between Hanne and Johann or create tension if they grieved differently. Communication and mutual support would be critical during this challenging time.

CONCLUSION

The birth and subsequent death of Johann Julius Riese just days later, while Friedrich was only one year old, would have created a profound impact on Hanne's emotional state and the family dynamics. While she would need to care for her surviving son, the shadow of grief would linger over their lives, shaping their interactions and emotional health in the months and years to come. Navigating the complexities of motherhood during this period would require resilience and support from her family and community.

August Ferdinand Koschnick[10]

August Ferdinand Koschnick was born into a fascinating period in 1824 in Löblau, West Prussia (today part of Poland). This era in the Danzig (Gdańsk) region, within the Kingdom of Prussia, was marked by significant social, political, and cultural changes.

1. Political Context

Part of Prussia: Löblau, along with much of West Prussia, had been part of the Prussian Kingdom since the partitions of Poland in the late 18th century. By 1824, Prussian rule had become firmly established, and the region was subject to Prussian law, governance, and bureaucratic efficiency. Prussia was emerging as a powerful state in Europe, known for its strict, centralized control, particularly in education and social policies.

Growing Nationalism: Prussia was beginning to foster a sense of German nationalism, aiming to unify the German-speaking states. This would eventually lead to the formation of the German Empire later in the century, but even by 1824, a German cultural and national identity was beginning to coalesce, impacting local communities.

2. SOCIAL AND CULTURAL Environment

Rural Village Life: Löblau and the surrounding region were primarily rural. Life here was likely centered around agriculture, with families working as farmers or laborers. The land was fertile, and the Vistula River provided a means for trade, so agriculture and small-scale trade were likely essential parts of daily life.

Religious Life: August's baptism in the Evangelical Church reflected the Protestant influence in the area, given that the Kingdom of Prussia was predominantly Lutheran after the Protestant Reformation. Church attendance and involvement were vital parts of life, and baptism was a significant rite of passage. The church served as a focal point for both religious and social gatherings in the community.

3. ECONOMIC CONDITIONS

Agrarian Economy: This region was heavily reliant on agriculture, with grain, wheat, rye, and barley as staple crops. Given that industrialization had yet to significantly alter rural areas, farming was labor-intensive, and families often relied on each other and their communities to meet agricultural demands.

Slow Industrial Changes: The early 1820s saw limited industrialization in Prussia. However, the beginnings of mechanized agriculture and textile production were emerging in some parts of Prussia, although these changes were slow to reach rural West Prussia.

4. DAILY LIFE AND FAMILY Structure

Family-Centered: Families were generally large, as children were needed to help on farms or with family trades. August would have been raised in a close-knit household, and the family would often be multigenerational, with grandparents and extended family living nearby.

Health and Mortality: Infant mortality rates were high, so the successful baptism of August was a cause for celebration, as it signified his survival through the fragile newborn period. However, general healthcare was minimal, with common illnesses potentially proving fatal, and much of medical care was based on traditional methods and local healers.

---

5. EDUCATION AND SOCIAL Mobility

Limited Education: While Prussia would later become known for its rigorous education system, formal schooling in rural West Prussia in 1824 was limited. Children like August may have had only basic schooling, often provided by the local church, if any. Literacy was not universal, and many rural families focused on skills relevant to farming and daily life.

Social Class and Hierarchy: Social mobility was limited. Most people remained in the social class into which they were born, working as farmers or artisans. However, Prussia's structured social hierarchy did offer some opportunities through military service or the church, but these were limited for the lower classes.

---

6. TECHNOLOGICAL ADVANCES and Limitations

Lack of Modern Conveniences: Daily life in 1824 would have been without the conveniences of later technology. Most household chores were done manually, and tasks like washing, cooking, and farming were labor-intensive. Transportation was limited to horse-drawn carts or walking, and travel between towns was challenging.

Early Developments: While basic inventions such as the mechanical spinning wheel had reached some rural areas, more complex technology, like the steam engine, was rare in agricultural regions.

CONCLUSION

For August Ferdinand Koschnick, born in rural West Prussia, life in 1824 would have revolved around family, church, and community within a structured Prussian state. His baptism in the Evangelical Church would have been a significant event, marking his formal entry into both religious life and the local society.

WHEN AUGUST FERDINAND Koschnick was just one year old, in 1825, matches were invented by English chemist John Walker. Although this invention was in its early stages, it marked the beginning of a simpler and more reliable way to create fire. Prior to this, fire was made using flint and steel, tinderboxes, or even by maintaining a continuous flame at home, which required consistent tending.

In rural areas like Löblau in Prussia, it would still be some time before matches became widely accessible. However, the eventual spread of this invention would be life-changing, making everyday tasks like lighting stoves, lanterns, and fires for cooking and warmth much easier and more efficient. For August's family and others in rural Prussia, the eventual availability of matches would simplify daily life, particularly in a time when reliable fire-making was essential.

WHEN AUGUST WAS 14 in 1838, photography became publicly available, starting with the daguerreotype process developed by Louis Daguerre in France. This breakthrough allowed people to capture images in a way that was previously unimaginable and led to a fascination with preserving likenesses and moments in time.

However, in rural Prussia, photography would not yet have been accessible to the average person. Early photography was expensive, time-consuming, and required specialized equipment. Initially, it was more likely to be used by the wealthy or within academic and scientific circles, as well as by those with the means to travel to larger cities where photographers had set up studios.

Over time, though, the spread of photography would open a new window into family memories and historical documentation, eventually reaching places like Löblau. This shift would allow people to create family portraits, document important life events, and preserve cultural history in ways previously limited to painted portraits and written records. For August, the spread of photography would have meant that his later years were likely documented and preserved in a way that had not been possible for previous generations.

AT 21 YEARS OLD, IN 1845, August witnessed the revolutionary patenting of the sewing machine by Elias Howe. This innovation promised to change the world of fabric and garment production drastically. Before the sewing machine, most clothing and household textiles were hand-sewn—a time-consuming task often requiring entire days to complete a single garment. Families, especially in rural areas like Löblau in West Prussia, relied on either handmade clothing or local seamstresses.

In August's community, where much of life involved hard physical labor and practical attire, the sewing machine's potential would have been significant. Though it took a few more years for sewing machines to become widely accessible and affordable, their eventual spread meant that households could save time and effort, allowing for greater productivity and even new business opportunities.

For people like August, the sewing machine would symbolize progress and modernization, leading to higher quality, more affordable clothing, and potentially transforming textile work into a faster, more efficient trade. This technology shift might have affected local industries and even household economies, as sewing moved from being a tedious, hand-done necessity to a task more easily managed with machines.

AUGUST AND RENATE'S wedding in 1849 in Löblau, West Prussia, would likely have been a modest and deeply traditional affair, reflecting both their religious values and the cultural customs of the time. Here's a glimpse into what their wedding might have been like:

Setting and Ceremony

The wedding would probably have taken place in the Evangelische Kirche Löblau, where August had been baptized. Protestant wedding ceremonies in 19th-century Prussia were often simple, focused on religious vows and blessings rather than lavish celebrations. The local pastor would have led the service, offering prayers and readings from the Bible to bless the couple's union. The ceremony would be in German, and hymns may have been sung by the congregation, contributing to a solemn yet joyful atmosphere.

After the church ceremony, there might have been a modest reception with close family and friends at a family home or local community hall. Such gatherings typically included a simple meal, possibly with local foods like rye bread, sausages, potatoes, pickled vegetables, and cakes or pastries if they could be afforded. A wedding toast with beer or wine may have marked the celebration, with toasts to the health and happiness of the couple.

Wedding Attire

August's Attire: As the groom, August would have likely worn his best clothes rather than a specially made suit, as was common for rural weddings of the period. His attire would have been formal yet practical, consisting of:

A dark wool coat or frock coat: This would be simple and durable, likely in black, dark gray, or brown, as dark colors were considered formal and suitable for special occasions.

A white linen shirt: Crisp and clean, this was a must for formal events.

Vest (waistcoat): He may have worn a vest in a solid, dark color or possibly with a subtle pattern. A vest was standard as it added formality and layers.

Trousers: Dark-colored, high-waisted trousers, possibly with braces (suspenders) to keep them in place.

Accessories: A cravat or necktie, usually white or another light color, to complete his outfit. He may have also worn a pocket watch if he owned one.

Shoes: Sturdy leather boots, well-shined for the occasion, as many rural men didn't own a separate pair of formal shoes.

RENATE'S ATTIRE: RENATE'S dress would have been similarly modest and practical, most likely in a traditional style rather than the elaborate white gowns that became popular later in the century. Her dress may have been in a muted color, such as dark blue, green, brown, or gray, as white was not yet common for weddings outside of wealthier circles. She may have added lace or ribbons as decoration, along with a simple bonnet or veil.

Community and Customs

Weddings in rural 19th-century Prussia were communal events, where families and close friends celebrated together. Traditional wedding customs might include blessings from family elders, as well as dancing if musicians were available. In a rural setting, community support played an essential role, so neighbors and friends may have contributed to the celebration by helping to prepare food or decorate the home.

As the couple married, they were stepping into their roles as future heads of a family in their community, which would come with responsibilities to both their household and the community at large. Their wedding would mark not just a personal union but a social event that bonded families and communities together.

WHEN AUGUST WAS 26 and his son, Gustav, was born on October 9, 1850, life in West Prussia was marked by a mixture of tradition and gradual change, as shifts in technology and society began influencing family life and the rural lifestyle.

Life as a New Father

As a father in rural West Prussia, August would likely take on a primary role in teaching his son practical skills to prepare him for work and responsibility in a rural setting. Raising children was a community effort as well, with extended family, church, and neighbors playing supporting roles. August would probably view his new role as a father as a chance to establish a legacy and secure his family's future.

Community and Religion

The Lutheran church, such as the Evangelische Kirche Löblau, played a central role in the lives of families like August's. Community members gathered here not only for worship but for social gatherings and events, including baptisms, weddings, and funerals. Gustav's birth would soon be followed by his baptism, a significant event for the family, likely performed within days or weeks after his birth. This sacrament would formally welcome Gustav into the church community, with family and possibly godparents present to support him spiritually.

Daily Life and Responsibilities

Agricultural work was often the backbone of life in rural West Prussia. If August and his family were engaged in farming or trades connected to the agrarian economy, his daily life would have been physically demanding, especially during harvest seasons. As a husband and father, he would have been primarily responsible for providing for his family, working long hours, and managing whatever land or livestock they might have had.

Social and Political Climate

In 1850, the German Confederation was undergoing shifts due to the events of the previous few years, especially the Revolutions of 1848, which had stirred calls for greater political rights and national unity. However, in a rural setting, much of the immediate impact of these events would be filtered through local authorities or seen in minor reforms rather than sweeping changes.

West Prussian communities held tightly to cultural traditions and values amid these changes. As a father, August would likely have been cautious about the uncertain times but also hopeful for his family's prospects. The growing availability of practical innovations, like photography (available for about a decade) and the early spread of ideas due to more widespread printed materials, may have been on the fringes of his awareness, showing the potential for future generations to see and experience life beyond the local village.

In summary, the arrival of his son Gustav would reinforce August's commitment to his family and faith in a world both grounded in tradition and quietly adapting to broader changes across Prussia and beyond.

———

AT 27, AUGUST BECAME a father to a daughter, Albertina Caroline, born on November 20, 1851. With two young children, he was likely focused on balancing family life with his work in Löblau, which may have been in agriculture or a similar local trade.

Family Dynamics and Parenting

With Albertina's birth, August and Renate faced the new challenges and joys of caring for an infant and a toddler. Renate would typically handle much of the day-to-day childcare, while August would focus on providing financial and material stability. In 1850s Prussia, raising a daughter differed from raising a son. Gustav, as the elder son, was expected to eventually learn skills needed for work outdoors or to take on trade skills, while Albertina would likely be prepared for domestic responsibilities and community-oriented roles.

Community and Religion

Albertina's arrival would be celebrated within their church community at Evangelische Kirche Löblau. Following her birth, she would likely be baptized there, marking an important religious and cultural moment for the family. This church remained central to their social and spiritual life, observing milestones, holidays, and educational events as Albertina and Gustav grew. Lutheran values of family, diligence, and community were likely guiding principles in their home.

Socioeconomic and Regional Context

Living in Löblau, August and Renate may have been alert to any regional changes that could impact their ability to support their growing family. While Löblau's rural life was relatively stable, the economic and industrial changes emerging across Prussia, including early industrialization, set the stage for future challenges or opportunities that could impact their children's futures. Though such changes were not yet prominent in smaller villages, they would eventually reach these regions.

The birth of Albertina likely reinforced August's dedication to creating a secure life for his family amid these gradual transformations, shaping his efforts and goals for the future in a changing world.

Renate (Jahnke) Koschnick[11]

———

Renate Jahnke's birth in 1823 places her in an era marked by significant transition for Germany, shaped by political, social, and economic forces that influenced life in both urban and rural settings.

Political and Social Climate

Germany was not yet a unified nation but a collection of independent states and territories under the loose confederation known as the German Confederation (Deutscher Bund), which was established after the Napoleonic Wars ended in 1815. Prussia and Austria were the dominant states within this confederation, often contending for influence. In this political landscape, regions like West Prussia, where Renate was born, were under the influence of Prussian rule, which involved a centralized and bureaucratic government, yet did not significantly change the day-to-day lives of those in rural areas.

Rural Life and Traditions

Renate's family likely lived in a village or small town where farming and agriculture were central. Most families depended on crops and livestock, with everyday life organized around the agricultural calendar. Rural communities placed a high value on family bonds and mutual support, as well as on religious practices that helped to maintain community cohesion. Lutheranism was deeply rooted in Prussia, and the local Evangelische Kirche Löblau would have played an essential role in family milestones, religious observances, and community gatherings.

Economic Changes

Economically, the early 19th century saw the beginning of the Industrial Revolution, although it primarily impacted cities and major towns rather than rural communities like those in West Prussia. However, the early stages of industrialization would slowly begin to affect all parts of society, bringing changes to production, trade, and eventually even to rural economies as demand for agricultural products increased. Small-scale artisans and craftsmen were common, with each village typically having blacksmiths, cobblers, and bakers who served the needs of the local population.

Everyday Life and Attire

For Renate's family, life would have been modest. Their clothing was typically homemade or locally made, using wool, linen, or cotton. Women wore simple dresses with aprons, and clothing was functional, suited to the demands of rural labor. Education, especially for girls, was limited, with basic literacy and practical skills prioritized to support household work. While boys were sometimes able to pursue apprenticeships or receive basic schooling, girls like Renate were likely taught domestic skills to prepare for family life and contribute to the household.

Regional Culture and Heritage

West Prussia, where Renate was born, held a mix of Polish and German influences, creating a unique cultural blend in the region's language, customs, and family structures. These communities took pride in local traditions, and customs such as folk music, dance, and seasonal festivals helped preserve a strong sense of identity despite the political changes around them.

In summary, Renate's early life in 1823 Prussia would have been shaped by a close-knit rural community, strong religious faith, and a modest but structured lifestyle grounded in the rhythms of agricultural life and family responsibilities.

WHEN RENATE WAS THREE years old and matches were invented in 1826, she was still in the early stages of childhood in her rural Prussian community. While innovations like matches represented small but significant advancements, their adoption would have been gradual, especially in rural areas. Before the widespread use of matches, people relied on methods like flint and steel or embers to start fires, which were essential for heating, cooking, and lighting in homes.

For Renate's family, matches would eventually become a valuable tool for convenience and safety, especially in managing hearth fires efficiently. But it's likely that, as a child, she would have seen her family using traditional methods for a few more years before matches became a more common household item. This small invention was one of many that symbolized the beginning of technological conveniences that would gradually transform daily life, even in rural communities like hers.

WHEN RENATE WAS 16 years old in 1839, photography became publicly available with the invention of the daguerreotype by Louis Daguerre. This marked a significant advancement in visual representation and communication, changing the way people documented their lives and experiences.

Impact on Renate's Life and Society

1. Cultural Shift: The availability of photography introduced a new medium for capturing and preserving memories. While Renate and her community may not have had immediate access to photography,

its introduction created a cultural shift toward visual representation, influencing how people saw themselves and their world.

---

2. FAMILY AND COMMUNITY Portraits: As photography gained popularity, it became common for families to commission portraits, capturing their likenesses for posterity. Renate's family, like many others, might have valued this new way to commemorate important life events, such as marriages, births, and other milestones.

---

3. SOCIAL STATUS AND Accessibility: Initially, photography was relatively expensive, limiting access to wealthier families or those living in urban areas. As the technology developed, prices gradually fell, allowing broader segments of society to engage with photography. For Renate, living in a rural area, this means that while her family may have eventually had the opportunity to have their portraits taken, it might not have been an immediate possibility.

---

4. INFLUENCE ON ART and Literature: The emergence of photography began to influence other art forms, inspiring painters and writers. Renate, if interested in the arts, might have found inspiration in the new visual medium, perhaps reflecting on how it could serve to document life in a more immediate way than painting or drawing.

---

5. TECHNOLOGICAL DEVELOPMENT: As photography evolved, it led to advancements in technology and techniques that would eventually make capturing images more accessible and widespread. Renate, growing up in an era of change, would witness the

gradual integration of photography into daily life, influencing her view of the world.

IN SUMMARY, RENATE'S teenage years coincided with the birth of photography, representing a significant cultural and technological shift. While its direct impact on her rural life might have been gradual, the broader implications of photography would shape societal interactions and the preservation of personal and family histories in the years to come.

WHEN RENATE WAS 23 years old in 1846, the sewing machine was patented by Elias Howe in the United States, marking a pivotal moment in the history of textile manufacturing and home sewing. Here's how this invention may have influenced her life and the broader context in Germany:

Impact on Renate and Society

1. Transformation of Textile Production: The invention of the sewing machine revolutionized the textile industry. Prior to its introduction, most clothing was handmade, which was time-consuming and labor-intensive. While the sewing machine would take some time to become widely adopted in Germany, its introduction hinted at a future where clothing production could become more efficient and accessible.

---

2. CHANGING GENDER Roles: The sewing machine began to alter the traditional roles associated with sewing. While sewing had been seen primarily as a domestic task performed by women, the sewing machine opened opportunities for women to engage in more

commercial sewing, potentially providing them with an income. For Renate, as she settled into adulthood and likely took on responsibilities of managing a household, the advent of the sewing machine could symbolize both the burden of increased domestic expectations and the potential for economic independence.

3. IMPACT ON HOME LIFE: In her household, if Renate or her family were to acquire a sewing machine, it would significantly reduce the time required for sewing clothing and household textiles. This could lead to a greater emphasis on fashion and the ability to produce garments more quickly. She may have also been involved in sewing for her family and neighbors, sharing skills that were important in maintaining a home.

4. ACCESS TO FASHION: The sewing machine paved the way for more rapid production of clothing, leading to an increase in availability and variety in fashion. Although Renate lived in a rural area, over time, she and her community would likely see changes in clothing styles and greater access to fashionable items, which may have influenced her choices in how she dressed and presented herself.

5. CULTURAL AND ECONOMIC Shifts: The broader implications of the sewing machine were felt across various social classes. While wealthier families could have access to ready-made clothing produced in factories, working-class families like Renate's would benefit from the ability to produce clothing more affordably and efficiently at home, fostering a sense of empowerment and self-sufficiency.

6. EDUCATIONAL OPPORTUNITIES: As the sewing machine became a household item, it could also lead to the establishment of sewing schools and classes, allowing women to learn new skills. This shift might inspire Renate to explore educational opportunities related to sewing, craftsmanship, or design.

IN SUMMARY, AT THE age of 23, Renate lived at a time when the sewing machine began to reshape the landscape of textile production and domestic life. This invention had the potential to empower women, streamline household tasks, and influence fashion trends, ultimately leading to broader societal changes that would be felt in the years to come.

RENATE JAHNKE AND AUGUST Ferdinand Koschnick's wedding in Löblau in 1849 would have reflected the customs and traditions of their time and culture, particularly within the Lutheran community in Germany. Here's an overview of what their wedding may have been like and what Renate might have worn:

Wedding Ceremony

1. Venue: The wedding likely took place in the local Evangelical Lutheran Church, which was a central part of community life. The church would have been decorated simply, as was customary, with perhaps a few flowers or greenery.

2. OFFICIANT: THE CEREMONY would have been conducted by a Lutheran pastor, who would lead them through traditional vows and

prayers, emphasizing the religious significance of marriage as a sacred covenant.

3. GUESTS: THE COUPLE would have been surrounded by family and friends, with attendance from their close relatives and community members. Weddings at that time were community events, and it was common for people to come together to celebrate.

4. RITUALS: THE CEREMONY might have included hymns sung by the congregation, readings from the Bible, and possibly a sermon on the meaning of marriage. The exchange of rings and vows would signify their commitment to one another.

5. RECEPTION: AFTER the ceremony, a celebration would likely follow at home or in a nearby hall, featuring food, drinks, and perhaps dancing. Traditional German foods might have been served, and there could have been speeches or toasts in honor of the couple.

RENATE'S ATTIRE

1. Dress Style: Renate's wedding dress would have been a reflection of the modest yet elegant styles of the time. Women in the mid-19th century often wore dresses with a fitted bodice and a full skirt. The fabric could range from simple cotton or linen for a more modest wedding to silk or satin for a more affluent celebration.

2. COLOR: ALTHOUGH white wedding dresses became popular later in the century, in the 1840s, brides often wore colored dresses or those made from more practical fabrics. Renate might have chosen a light color such as pale blue or pink, which were considered appropriate for a wedding.

———

3. ACCESSORIES: SHE might have worn a simple veil or a decorative headpiece, possibly adorned with flowers. Jewelry would likely be understated, perhaps featuring a necklace or earrings passed down from family.

———

4. FOOTWEAR: HER SHOES would have been made of leather or fabric, designed for comfort and practicality, suitable for both the ceremony and the reception.

———

5. ADDITIONAL ELEMENTS: It was common for brides to carry a bouquet, which could include locally sourced flowers or herbs. The bouquet might have been tied with a ribbon that complemented her dress.

———

CULTURAL SIGNIFICANCE

The wedding ceremony would have been a significant event in Renate and August's lives, marking the beginning of their life together as a married couple. The Lutheran tradition would have imbued the occasion with a sense of spiritual importance, reflecting their faith and commitment to one another in the eyes of God and their community.

Overall, Renate's wedding would have been a blend of religious significance, community celebration, and personal style, with traditions that reflect the customs of mid-19th century Germany.

———

RENATE KOSCHNICK, AT 27 years old when her son Gustav was born on October 9, 1850, would have experienced a significant and transformative event in her life. Here's an exploration of how she might have been affected by becoming a mother:

Emotional Impact

1. Joy and Fulfillment: The birth of her first child would likely have brought her immense joy and a sense of fulfillment. Becoming a mother was often viewed as a primary role for women during this time, and having a healthy child could be a source of pride and happiness.

———

2. BONDING: THE INITIAL bond between Renate and her newborn would have been strong. The nurturing instinct to care for and protect Gustav would have taken precedence, and she might have experienced deep emotional attachment.

———

3. ANXIETY AND RESPONSIBILITY: With the arrival of a child comes new responsibilities. Renate may have felt anxious about her ability to raise Gustav well and ensure his health and well-being, especially considering the high infant mortality rates of the time.

———

PHYSICAL IMPACT

1. Postpartum Recovery: The physical demands of childbirth would require Renate to recover, and she may have experienced fatigue and the challenges of adjusting to her new role. Childbirth in the 19th century often came with risks, and her recovery would be crucial for both her and her baby.

2. CHANGES IN ROUTINE: Her daily routine would have changed significantly. Caring for a newborn would require much of her time and attention, affecting her previous household responsibilities and any social activities she might have engaged in.

SOCIAL IMPACT

1. Community Support: In a tight-knit community like Löblau, Renate might have received support from other women, family members, and neighbors. This communal assistance could have included help with child-rearing, cooking, and household chores.

2. INCREASED SOCIAL Expectations: With motherhood, there may have been heightened expectations from society regarding her behavior and responsibilities as a mother. Renate would likely feel the pressure to adhere to the norms of motherhood, which included nurturing and educating her child.

3. ROLE WITHIN THE Family: Renate's role within her family would evolve as she transitioned to motherhood. Her relationship with August might also change, as they would need to navigate their

partnership in parenting together, potentially strengthening their bond as they shared responsibilities.

***

LONG-TERM CONSIDERATIONS

1. Future Children: The birth of Gustav could have influenced Renate's decisions about future pregnancies. Families often expanded quickly in this era, and she may have started thinking about how many children she wanted and how to manage their upbringing.

***

2. LEGACY AND IDENTITY: As a mother, Renate would begin to shape her identity around her role in raising Gustav. The values, beliefs, and traditions she instilled in him would reflect her own upbringing and experiences.

***

IN SUMMARY, RENATE Koschnick's life would have changed dramatically upon the birth of her son Gustav. The experience would bring joy, new responsibilities, and a shift in her identity, with profound emotional and social implications as she navigated motherhood in mid-19th century Germany.

***

THE DEATH OF GUSTAV Koschnick on January 13, 1851, would have had a profound and heartbreaking impact on Renate and her family. Here's an exploration of how she might have been affected by this loss:

Emotional Impact

1. Grief and Mourning: Renate would likely have experienced intense grief following Gustav's passing. The loss of a child is one of the most devastating experiences a parent can face, and she would have felt profound sorrow and possibly despair.

2. SHOCK AND DISBELIEF: Given that Gustav was born only a few months earlier, Renate might have felt shock at the suddenness of his death. It is common for parents to struggle with disbelief when faced with such a tragedy, questioning how something so painful could happen.

3. ISOLATION: DURING this period, societal norms often discouraged open expressions of grief. Renate may have felt isolated in her sorrow, struggling to find comfort and support from others while navigating her pain.

PHYSICAL IMPACT

1. Health Consequences: The emotional turmoil of losing a child can have physical consequences, potentially leading to stress-related health issues. Renate might have experienced fatigue, changes in appetite, or difficulty sleeping as she processed her grief.

2. MATERNAL ROLE REASSESSMENT: The loss could cause Renate to reassess her identity and her role as a mother. She may have felt inadequate or guilty for not being able to protect her child, impacting her mental well-being.

SOCIAL IMPACT

1. Support Systems: In a close-knit community like Löblau, Renate might have found some support through friends and family who could empathize with her loss. However, societal expectations of stoicism might have made it challenging for her to openly express her grief.

2. COMMUNITY RESPONSE: The community may have held memorial services or provided condolences, but Renate could have felt that no one could truly understand the depth of her loss. The customs surrounding mourning during this time might have been both comforting and stifling.

3. IMPACT ON MARRIAGE: The death of Gustav could have affected Renate's relationship with August. Grieving parents sometimes experience strain in their marriages as they process their loss differently. They may have had to navigate differing coping mechanisms and emotions.

LONG-TERM CONSIDERATIONS

1. Future Children: The death of Gustav might have influenced Renate's feelings about having more children in the future. She could have felt hesitant or fearful about pregnancy and childbirth, knowing the risks involved.

2. LEGACY OF GRIEF: The memory of Gustav would likely remain with Renate, shaping her perspectives on motherhood and family. She might have kept his memory alive through stories or rituals, impacting how she viewed her subsequent children (if she had any).

---

3. RESILIENCE AND GROWTH: While the loss would be devastating, many parents find ways to cope and rebuild after such tragedies. Renate might have discovered strength and resilience she didn't know she had, ultimately impacting how she approached life and motherhood in the future.

IN SUMMARY, THE DEATH of Gustav would have had a profound effect on Renate Koschnick, causing deep emotional pain, potential health issues, social challenges, and long-lasting implications for her identity and family life. The loss of a child is a significant life event that often reshapes a parent's life in countless ways.

RENATE'S EXPERIENCE following the birth of her daughter, Albertina Caroline, on November 20, 1851, would have been shaped by her previous loss of Gustav just ten months earlier. Here's an exploration of how her new role as a mother to Albertina might have affected her emotionally, socially, and physically:

Emotional Impact

1. Bittersweet Joy: While the arrival of a new child would typically bring joy and excitement, for Renate, it would likely be accompanied by bittersweet feelings. The joy of having a daughter might be overshadowed by the recent grief over Gustav's death.

2. FEAR AND ANXIETY: Renate might have experienced heightened anxiety about Albertina's health and well-being. Having lost one child, she could have been overly cautious or worried about any signs of illness or distress in her new baby.

3. HOPE AND HEALING: The birth of Albertina could also represent a glimmer of hope and a chance for healing. Renate might have poured her love and affection into her new daughter, finding solace in nurturing a new life.

PHYSICAL IMPACT

1. Postpartum Recovery: Renate would be going through physical recovery from childbirth while still grieving Gustav. The physical demands of caring for a newborn can be overwhelming, especially when compounded by emotional fatigue.

2. NURSING AND BONDING: Nursing Albertina could provide Renate with a sense of purpose and connection. This nurturing aspect might help her cope with her earlier loss, as she forms a bond with her new daughter.

SOCIAL IMPACT

1. Community Support: The arrival of a new child often brings community support. Friends and neighbors might have offered

assistance or congratulations, helping Renate feel connected and supported during this challenging time.

---

2. COMPARISON WITH Gustav: Renate may have found herself comparing Albertina to Gustav, reflecting on how different their lives were. This comparison could evoke both sorrow and joy as she navigated her feelings about her children.

---

3. IMPACT ON MARRIAGE: The dynamics of Renate's relationship with August could have changed with the arrival of Albertina. They might have found a renewed sense of purpose as parents, but there could also be challenges in managing their grief while raising a new child.

LONG-TERM CONSIDERATIONS

1. Motherhood: Renate's experience with Albertina could transform her view of motherhood. She might approach parenting with more caution, cherishing each moment but also fearing potential loss.

---

2. LEGACY OF LOSS: The memory of Gustav might shape how Renate raises Albertina. She may emphasize health and well-being, potentially instilling a sense of resilience in her daughter.

---

3. FUTURE CHILDREN: Depending on how she copes with Albertina's arrival, Renate might be more open or hesitant to having

more children. If she finds joy in motherhood again, it could encourage her to expand her family further.

IN SUMMARY, THE BIRTH of Albertina Caroline in the wake of Gustav's death would bring a complex mix of emotions for Renate Koschnick. She would likely experience both joy and fear, along with a renewed sense of purpose as she navigated the challenges of motherhood. This period could be a time of healing and resilience, shaping her identity as a mother moving forward.

FOR FURTHER RESEARCH:

MOSES HESS[1]

MOSES HESS'S BACKGROUND[2]

MOSES HESS[3]

MOSES HESS'S INFORMATION[4]

MARTIN LUTHER[5]

LUTHERANS IN GERMANY[6]

MUST-SEE LUTHERAN CHURCHES IN GERMANY[7]

[1] https://www.wikitree.com/wiki/Hess-6738

[2] https://www.wikitree.com/wiki/Hess-6737

[3] https://www.wikitree.com/genealogy/Hess-Family-Tree-6740

[4] https://www.wikitree.com/wiki/Rophinski-1

[5] https://www.wikitree.com/wiki/Unknown-700090

[6] https://www.wikitree.com/wiki/Riese-134

[7] https://www.wikitree.com/wiki/Riese-135

[8] https://www.wikitree.com/wiki/Melhorn-173

[9] https://www.wikitree.com/wiki/Riese-136

[10] https://www.wikitree.com/wiki/Koschnick-1

[11] https://www.wikitree.com/wiki/Jahnke-260

Don't miss out!

Visit the website below and you can sign up to receive emails whenever Angeline Gallant publishes a new book. There's no charge and no obligation.

https://books2read.com/r/B-A-QGSI-GUGTB

BOOKS 2 READ

Connecting independent readers to independent writers.

Also by Angeline Gallant

A Dragon's Diary
Dreaming of Dragons

Calling Her Heart
Whisper of the Heart
No Turning Back
Forsake Me Not
Hear My Cry

FORGET ME NOT
Victoria, Ontario's Babies 1894 - 1895

Guardian of the Heart
Fallen Petals

Keeper Of Secrets
A Lady's Secret

Kingston's Love Chronicles
Springtime Promises

Midnight's Awakening
Heart of the Storm
Walking Through The Storm
Walking Through The Storm
Heart of the Storm

Secrets of the Underworld
Deklan's Dragons

Tell My Story Collection
Tell My Story: Germany 1851
Tell My Story: England 1852

The Dervock Legacy
Echoes of Dervock

The Grave Whisperer
Cataraqui United Church Cemetery
Wedding Bells in Kingston, Ontario, Canada 1923
St. Paul's Anglican Churchyard Kingston, Ontario, Canada A-B

St. Paul's Anglican Churchyard, Kingston, Ontario, Canada C - D
St. Paul's Anglican Churchyard, Kingston, Ontario, Canada G - H
St. Paul's Anglican Churchyard, Kingston, Ontario, Canada J - N
St. Paul's Anglican Churchyard, Kingston, Ontario, Canada O - R
St. Paul's Anglican Churchyard, Kingston, Ontario, Canada S - T
St. Paul's Anglican Churchyard, Kingston, Ontario T - Z
Small Graveyards & Burial Grounds: Kingston, Ontario, Canada
Cataraqui United Church Cemetery 1
Cataraqui United Church Cemetery 2
Cataraqui United Church Cemetary 3
Cataraqui United Church Cemetery 4
Cataraqui United Church Cemetery 5
Beth Israel Cemetery
Cataraqui United Church Cemetery 6

The Timeless Veil
Eternal Devotion

The Wolf Whisperer Series
Journey of the Heart
Cry of a Warrior
Wolf Whisperer volumes 1 & 2
Endless White
The Wolf Whisperer volumes 1 & 2

Timeless
The Time Keeper's Sanctuary

Timeless Whispers of Dervock Saga
Secrets of Dervock

Standalone
Winds of Change vol 1-3

Watch for more at https://www.goodreads.com/author/show/19703964.Angeline_Gallant.

About the Author

Angeline Gallant is a Geneology addict who loves to work on her family tree and help others with theirs. This passion for history plays a huge role in her books as well.

An Old Stock Canadian and a homeschooling mother living in Canada, Angeline is determined to leave her own special mark on the world through her work, her child, and her writing.

Angeline is an author on Goodreads. If you follow her account on Goodreads, she will follow back.

Read more at https://www.goodreads.com/author/show/19703964.Angeline_Gallant.